MOUNTAINS OF THE MOON

PATRICK SYNGE

MOUNTAINS OF THE MOON

WATERSTONE · LONDON

Waterstone & Co. Limited
49 Hay's Mews
London W1X 7RT

First published in Great Britain 1937.
Travel Book Club edition 1938.

This edition first published by
Waterstone & Co. Limited 1985.
By kind permission of Mrs M. G. Synge.

ISBN 0 947752 40 4

Front cover: 'The Seventh Nyamgasani Lake,' by
Stuart Somerville. © The Estate of the artist.
Reproduced by kind permission of
John Somerville and Mrs Woodhouse.

Back cover: Helichrysum Guilelmii T.7789 from
Botanical Magazine vol. 127. Reproduced with permission.
Copyright of the Trustees of the Royal Botanic Gardens,
Kew © 1985.

Cover Design by Carol Brickley at Boldface.

Printed and bound in Great Britain by
Richard Clay (The Chaucer Press) Ltd,
Bungay, Suffolk.

Distributed (except in USA) by
Thames and Hudson Ltd

To

G . L . R . H .

'Around this bay the Anthropophagi Aethiopians dwell, and from there towards the West are the Mountains of the Moon from which the lakes of the Nile receive snow water.'

Ptolemy, Book 4, chap. viii.

FOREWORD

Patrick Synge, my father, was born in London in 1910, the son of Edward Synge, artist and engraver. He was educated at Rugby and then at Corpus Christi College Cambridge, where he studied Natural Sciences.

He had just graduated from Cambridge, and was twenty-two, when he was offered the post of assistant botanist and photographer to the Oxford University Sarawak Expedition (1932-1933). He then joined the British Museum Expedition to the mountain regions of equatorial East Africa in 1934, in the company of Dr. George Taylor (later to become Sir George Taylor and Director of Kew). *Mountains of the Moon* is as much my father's personal account of that expedition as it is an official record; it shows his love of plants and his gift for inspired observation. It is particularly apt that the cover illustration of this new edition should be a reproduction of the evocative painting 'The Seventh Nyamgasani Lake' by his close friend Stuart Somerville, the expedition's artist.

My father had great hopes that many of the plants he collected would become established garden plants in England. Two plants – Canarina Eminii (the bell flower) and Choananthus crytanthiflorus – were successful, and the Royal Horticultural Society (RHS) gave each of these an Award of Merit when my father exhibited them at Chelsea in 1938. However, by the time he published *Plants with Personality*, in 1939, it was already becoming evident that few, if any, of his other introductions would prosper here. Of Lobelia Wollastonii he wrote, 'several of these are rooting and I hope may yet succeed, although I cannot claim that they grow with any great vigour. Perhaps the beautiful silvery-blue spike is destined only to remain a memory with me until I visit the mountain again', and of Senecio brassica, 'for some time we had several plants of this species growing quite vigorously here in Surrey, but unfortunately they have now all died.'

He continued to grow some of the plants in his own garden, but only two survived into recent times and they did not achieve their natural size. A plant of the giant Lobelia gibberoa continued, in a pot, until the early seventies: more attractive was a fine specimen of Impatiens elegantissima, now considered a sub-species of I. tinctoria, which grew in open ground until a few years ago and fortunately survives in a neighbour's garden, dying back to the base each year. This book is the best memorial to the plants found on the expedition.

After serving in North Africa and Italy during the war, my father resumed his botanical and literary career, becoming editor of the Journal, and of other publications of the RHS, in 1945. He completed the Society's *Dictionary of Gardening* and its supplement – a mammoth task – as well as writing many other books, including *Collins Guide to Bulbs* (1961), *In Search of Flowers* (1973), *Flowers and Colour in Winter* (1974) and *The Gardens of Devon and Cornwall* (1977). He was joint author, with Roy Hay, of the best-selling *Dictionary of Garden Plants in Colour*. The RHS honoured my father with the Veitch Memorial Gold Medal in 1957, and later with the Lyttel Lily Cup and the Victoria Medal of Honour. He died in 1982.

Much of the area explored by the British Museum Expedition of 1934 was designated a World Heritage Site by UNESCO in 1979. The higher areas of the Ruwenzori remain physically unaffected by man, and the waters from those mountains even now sustain most of Egypt as they always have done. The 'monstrous and unearthly landscape' that my father described in this book still keeps its strange botanical inhabitants to itself since, even with the greatest care, they would not flourish in England. It is, then, so satisfying to see this book in print again.

HUGH SYNGE

INTRODUCTION

A grey mist made a fitting background for the most monstrous and unearthly landscape that I have ever seen. Vague outlines of peaks and precipices towered around us. Here were plants which seemed more like ghosts of past ages than ordinary trees and herbs. They appeared as a weird and terrible dream to me, a botanist and hunter of strange plants. It all seemed unreal, like some imaginary reconstruction of life in a long past geological age, or even upon another planet. Our own familiar common herbs seemed to have gone mad. We saw groundsels, swollen and distorted with woody trunks twenty feet in height, lobelias like gigantic blue and green obelisks, heathers mighty as great trees. Most alpine plants are reduced to extreme dwarfness, but these have rushed to the opposite extreme and exhibit an exaggerated gigantism. On the ground grew a thick carpet of mosses. Some were brilliant yellow, others deep crimson in colour. Every shade of green was represented. The tree trunks were also clothed in thick moss, often tussocked into the semblance of faces, while from their branches dangled long streamers of a pale, sulphurous yellow lichen, the old man's beard.

A solitary figure stood on the crest of the ridge. For a moment he stood erect and silent, silhouetted darkly against the light. Far away, on a bank of cloud below, appeared his shadow, a spectral giant. A grey blanket, knotted over his shoulders, hung toga-like around him. In his hand he carried a long staff. This was the man we came to know as the Rain Man of Ruwenzori. From his waist dangled the whistle which he blew to keep away the rain. We had no rain.

He seemed to us a symbol of this strange place, a symbol of the uncanny influence which it exerted on us, its blackness, its unearthly power. Here the silence was the voice. It is good to be able to escape sometimes from the ordinary world; this strange mountain carried us into a dreamland which was often a fairyland, occasionally a nightmare.

A moment, and then the spell was broken. Into this world of unhuman fantasy came a brief interlude of humanity. One by one a long line of black figures came up on to the ridge and joined the 'Rain' man. Laughs and jokes broke the silence as they dropped their loads on to the carpet of moss; here part of a tent, here a bag of flour, there a bulging plant press or a square insect box labelled 'British Museum (Natural History)', there an artist's case and easel. Of such was our expedition. Gratefully they sank down on to the damp feather bed which made the ground here. It is perpetually damp, even though by a miracle there had been no rain. When we arrived, long pipes had already been lit, passing from man to man. We were greeted with a cheerful throng of black faces: 'Weyballe Bwana, Weyballe, Well done,' they exclaimed, pleased at our arrival. We returned the compliment to them, far more deserving of it than ourselves. We have collected on the way a pile of plants and insects, and paused to take a photograph whenever tired, while they have carried heavy loads, skilfully balanced on their heads, over the most difficult ground. The giant leaves were quickly placed in a press, the seeds in little envelopes, and we too sank back luxuriantly into the moss. After a quarter of an hour of ease the procession started again. 'Kwenda, Kwenda, tugende, let us go'; loads were quickly lifted on to heads, and so we moved on towards the snow peak which could dimly be seen in front of us. We were standing almost on the Equator, yet it was as cold as a really cold winter's day in England, and a little ahead there was permanent snow and ice.

Classical writers have told of a source of the Nile lying in a silvery mountain south of Ethiopia and in the centre of Africa. Ptolemy wrote of this place as 'The Mountains of the Moon'. Herodotus wove an attractive legend about it. Arab writers also wrote of a silvery mountain. Yet no personal

record of a visit to 'The Mountains of the Moon' has survived.
It is doubtful whether any of the Mediterranean peoples did
ever visit any of the Equatorial mountains of Africa in
classical times. For many centuries there remained alive the
story of 'The Mountains of the Moon', a legend, mysterious
and alluring. Throughout the Middle Ages the story
remained. Then, towards the end of the last century,
explorers discovered in Central Africa such a mountain
which they called Ruwenzori, from the African word
'Rwenzura', the rainy mountain. From her snows water
flows into the Nile. For most of the year her top is clouded in
mist, and it is possible to pass close to her base without
perceiving that there is a great mountain within a few miles.
Stanley did so. Then he returned and saw white peaks rising
above the clouds. His porters told him that it was salt up
there in the sky. Stanley hailed this mountain 'Ruwenzori' as
'The Mountains of the Moon' mentioned by Ptolemy, and
the name has stuck to the mountain in spite of much
controversy.*

A short expedition organized for the study of the plants
and animals of one valley in this great mountain Ruwenzori
was an experience which I will not quickly forget. The first
part of this book will deal with these experiences, visual,
mental and physical.

Ruwenzori is a mass of high mountain situated right on the
Equator and almost in the centre of Africa. The boundary
line between Uganda and the Belgian Congo actually passes
longitudinally along her highest watershed. The Equator
divides her transversely.

Ruwenzori cannot be considered as a single mountain. It
is over fifty miles in length, and has six main snow-topped
masses, separated by gorges several thousand feet deep.
These peaks have been dignified by the name of Mounts,
Mt. Baker, Mt. Stanley, Mt. Luigi di Savoia, etc. They stand
out high from the main massif. It is, indeed, almost a range.

*See Appendix I.

Ruwenzori is not a volcanic mass as are the other great mountains of Equatorial Africa. She consists of very ancient rocks, squeezed up at some past time of geological activity like a section from an orange. Many of these contain mica schists and sparkle like great slabs of silver in the sun. This adds to her glory.

The mountain has not in the past been neglected by explorers, but even now there are valleys largely unknown and yet unvisited. All the highest peaks have now been climbed, but so infrequently that a new ascent is still a notable event; while the less ambitious traveller can climb many minor peaks which are still virgin, and traverse country so fantastic and beautiful that it will always remain with him as a cherished memory.

The first great expedition to explore and to map the higher zones of the mountain was that of the Duke of the Abruzzi in 1906. In the same year came also the first British Museum Expedition; ours was the second. Since 1920 the most notable expeditions have been those of Dr. Noel Humphreys, who first made an aerial reconnaissance from the Uganda side, and of the Belgian Comte de Grunne from the western Congo side. Practically all expeditions have recorded bad weather. Nearly all the other high Equatorial mountains can be visited as a holiday trip, but Ruwenzori claims an expedition, carefully planned, organized and equipped.

When a friend stationed as a Government entomologist in Uganda wrote to me and suggested a small expedition to carry on his study of the relations between the flora and fauna of Ruwenzori and the other high Equatorial mountains of East Africa, I felt much tempted. He also pointed out that such an expedition was now feasible without great expense, since there were good roads in Uganda by which we could approach the mountains, where former explorers had walked from the coast.

At that time I was still engaged with a tripos examination

at Cambridge. Immediately the tripos was over I had arranged to leave England for seven months with an expedition controlled by the Oxford Exploration Club and organized by my friend Tom Harrisson to visit Mt. Dulit in the interior of Borneo. So the African expedition had to be postponed. However, the expedition to Borneo even surpassed my expectations in interest and whetted my appetite for more adventures of the same kind.

It was three years before I was able to set out for Africa with two friends, Stuart Somerville, artist, and John Ford, entomologist. Ford had also been a member of the Borneo Expedition. Out of such small beginnings grew the second British Museum Expedition to the East African Mountains. Drs. Edwards and Taylor, appointed by the Trustees as joint official leaders, followed us in four months' time.

The purposes of the expedition were both systematic and ecological: that is, we wanted to find out what plants grew on these mountains, and to collect specimens of them pressed for the Herbaria at the British Museum and at Kew. We wanted also to find out the associations in which they grew on the mountain, and as far as possible something of the conditions under which they grew.

We also wanted to make a comparative study of several of the mountains, although we had a very short time in which to do this: in my case a year, in the case of Edwards and Taylor only six months. Ruwenzori was our main objective, but we also visited Mount Elgon, Mount Kenya, the Aberdare Mountains and several of the Birunga volcanoes.

All these mountains stand up like islands from the surrounding warmer plain, islands of peculiar vegetation, which would seem to be a relic of a flora formerly much more widely spread. It is a curious fact that many of the genera on these mountains, and even a few of the actual species, are similar to those found in England. High up on Ruwenzori we found a white sanicle similar to that found in many English woods, while on Elgon there was a little violet with mauve flowers very like our wild English violet, though without any scent. The same curious affinities were observed in the insects, particularly the insects associated with the giant plants. Both plants and insects are totally different from those found in all other parts of Africa, with the exception of some of the higher parts of Abyssinia.

It seems probable that in former geological ages there were periods in which central Africa was very much colder and wetter than it is at present, and that the lakes extended over far greater areas. In such a climate types of plants and animals which now inhabit the temperate, and even the sub-arctic regions, could live comfortably right on the Equator in a land which is now much too warm and dry for them. Then the glaciation in the north retreated. The icecaps on the African mountains also decreased, and in some cases, for example Mt. Elgon, they actually disappeared, maybe at the same time as the Ice Age in Europe retreated, maybe later. As the icecaps retreated up the mountains we may assume that the cold-loving plants followed them until they reached their present positions. The mountain floras do not to-day really begin till a height of 7,000 feet is reached. Thus we may assume that the different mountain floras became isolated from one another and evolved separately. Each mountain top is a little garden where evolution may have proceeded uninfluenced by the rest of lower Africa. But allowing that all this is true, and it is difficult to think of any other explanation of these curious floras, we would expect to find fossils allied to present-day mountain plants in the lower lands. None have so far been found, but this cannot be taken as proof that the plants were never there.

The mountains are separated from each other by a considerable distance, and there is no present bridge by which plants could pass from one to the other. Yet on each mountain there is the same general aspect and zonation of the flora, the same peculiar gigantism in certain genera, although there is variation among the actual species. This present variation would make distribution of the plants by migratory birds unlikely as a factor acting at present. Only one species of giant lobelia is common to all the mountains. This was the lowest and also the largest species that we found, but in Tanganyika, close to the Amani station, there is another species which grows as low as 3,000 feet. I think that it is significant that the greater variation occurs higher up the mountains. Thus these peculiar plants open up innumerable questions which are still unsolved. How did they get on to these mountains, or did they develop there? What caused their extraordinary gigantism? How fast do they grow, how long do they live, and under what conditions do they now live?

On the origin of the gigantism no one has been able to produce any really satisfactory theory. We can only say that it would appear to be due to the complement of the rather peculiar environmental conditions present – a low temperature, but one that is moderately constant throughout the year, a very high and constant humidity, and a high ultra-violet light intensity due to the altitude and the Equatorial position. But we do not really know. In England I have found that these plants grow more actively in the winter. Warmth acts as an inhibiting factor. There is nothing in the behaviour of the particular genera Lobelia and Senecio in other parts of the world to adduce an inherent character of gigantism in them, rather the opposite when we think of the little blue Lobelia cultivated in our English gardens.

We hoped to bring back seeds of some of the giant Lobelias and Groundsels, in order to see whether they could be established in English gardens. Although in summer there are flowers of many kinds to make our gardens bright, in winter there is a singular bareness and lack of colour. This has recently been improved by the introduction of many fine plants from China and the Himalayas. But any plant that will look green, and maybe flower, in the winter in England is valuable. Some of the plants from the mountains of Equatorial Africa are so vast, almost statuesque in their habits, that they would decorate any landscape. They are, moreover, evergreen, and a very vivid green too. Growing up by the snows, sometimes with actual snow on their leaves, many withstand considerable frost. They grow, too, in an atmosphere which is almost perpetually damp, so there seemed a chance that they might do well in English gardens.

In addition to the gigantic Lobelias and Senecios, there are many attractive Everlastings (*Helichrysums*), many of far more grace and charm than those usually cultivated in England. There are tree St. John's worts (*Hypericum*), red-hot pokers (*Kniphofia*), and many delightful bulbous plants, such as *Crinum*, *Gladiolus*, and *Romulea*. However, the feasts of pure colour which are to be seen in the Alps, and also, I believe, in the Himalayas, are absent from these mountains. It is in the discovery of individual plants that the botanist obtains his chief pleasure.

CONTENTS

CHAPTER I

THE ROAD TO RUWENZORI

A ROAD, winding and twisting round every little green hill, curling sometimes almost back on itself, led to Fort Portal and to Ruwenzori, the mountain which had always seemed to me by far the most attractive and romantic in Africa. Along this we drove one morning in December.

The most frequent route up to the snows follows first the Mubuku valley and then its tributary, the Bujuku. For the ascent of the higher peaks this is still probably the best. Practically all the recent expeditions from the Uganda side have ascended this way. From the west another route, that of the Butawu valley, has been opened recently by the Belgian Expedition under the Comte de Grunne.

We aimed at investigating two hitherto almost unknown valleys ascending from the south and the southeast. These were the Nyamgasani and the Namwamba. Dr. Scott Elliott, in his book of African travel, tells of a very hurried ascent made up the Namwamba as far as 13,000 feet. Otherwise we knew of no one who had been up that way. We did not know of any ascents of the Nyamgasani, but in the highest part Dr. Humphreys had discovered from the air a string of eight lakes. These he had subsequently visited, crossing over a high pass from another valley; descending the Nyamgasani valley as far as 12,000 feet and making the first ascents of Weismann peak, 15,165 feet, the highest point of Mt. Luigi di Savoia, and of Mt. Watamagufu, which lay between the Nyamgasani and Namwamba valleys. He had only been in the valley two days, on both of which he had experienced very bad weather, but he had reported that these included the largest lakes in the massif, and he strongly recommended us to go there.

We decided to split the expedition into two parties, so as to cover as much ground as possible in the short time available. We went to Ruwenzori during the Uganda dry season, at the end of December and January when all else was dusty and the air was thick with smoke from innumerable grass fires.

Former travellers have, almost without exception, recorded continual rain, mist, cold, hail, sleet, snow, and every other form of damp misery. Dr. Humphreys had told us that he thought there was no kind of regular dry weather on the mountain, but had advised us to try midwinter or midsummer, both seasons which do not really exist in Uganda. Hancock had ascended the Mubuku and Bujuku valleys at midsummer and had experienced some fine days. The mountain had generally been climbed during the other months, and its reputation for rain and cold was very evil. Perhaps our experience may help to give it a slightly better name.

Edwards and Taylor decided to go to the Namwamba valley. They had been offered a base at the Kilembe copper mine, which is just at the foot of this valley. Here lived several Europeans and a large staff, but they had never made a path right up the valley behind them. E. G. Gibbins, of the Uganda Medical Department, went with them. They were also able to secure for a short time the services of George Oliver, who had accompanied Humphreys on at least one of his journeys. They started off first, leaving Kampala early in December with a lorry full of stores and equipment.

The Nyamgasani was left to a second party which consisted of Somerville, David Buxton, and myself. A. S. Thomas, the botanist from the Uganda Agricultural Laboratories at Kampala, had intended to come with us, and had even come back early from leave for the purpose.

4

A few days after his return, and only three days before our intended start, he became ill with typhoid fever. It was, indeed, hard luck for him, besides being a severe blow to our organization. Buxton, luckily, was able to fill his place at short notice. He was an entomologist, and was engaged on locust investigation at the time. He had been longer in the country than either of us and knew some Swahili, which proved valuable. We had seen much of him recently, since, like us, he often made a base at Hancock's house in Kampala. We were very glad that he would be able to come with us.

Somerville and I had by now been in the country for five months, and had already visited several of the other mountains. So we thought we knew a little about the matter—only very little though. Most unfortunately, John Ford, our original companion, had now to return to England to resume his research scholarship at Oxford, and was not able to come with us to Ruwenzori.

Several days were occupied in the preparation of the safari. The heavy equipment was dispatched on the same lorry as that of the other party, who promised to dump it for us at Kilembe. Our cars were much overladen before we left, first Somerville and myself, then Buxton a day later. Both our cars were very ancient, mine, a great Vauxhall tourer about six years old, held quite a lot but not nearly so much as Buxton's smaller Ford with its box body. Altogether this was a more serviceable type of car for our rough purposes.

We had been warned that no food of any kind could be obtained on the mountain. We must be prepared to feed both our porters and ourselves for six weeks. Bulo flour is the main item of food of the porters, and there was a tradition that porters on Ruwenzori would not eat anything else. Bulo is derived from a species of *Eleusine*, a millet. So we wired to an Indian contractor at Fort Portal to have an ample supply of Bulo flour ready for

5

us. Uganda is now, in most parts, a very civilized country, with good roads, posts and telegraphs. Unfortunately, when we arrived there, we learnt that this year there had been a shortage of bulo and he was only able to supply us with a small quantity. This seemed a heavy obstacle, but we decided to take what was available and to try to get more on the way. For our boys we took a supply of rice, since green bananas, their usual food, would have proved far too heavy and they would not be able to eat flour like the porters. For ourselves, among other things, Christmas puddings in tins, hoping to spend a real old-fashioned English Christmas up by the snow. However, we didn't get there in time. Still the plum puddings were very acceptable, and for their weight they seemed excellent food value for the higher zones. Edwards was able to make over to us some of the tinned and dried foods he had brought out from England and also a case of chocolate, one of several given by Cadbury's. This proved invaluable. It is certainly one of the best things to take on mountain expeditions, and it is extremely expensive to buy throughout East Africa. We took tents, all we could muster, some for ourselves to be used as proper tents, and some for the porters to make communal shelters rigged over poles. We took all the warm clothes we possessed or which we could borrow. Remembering our experience when lost in the mist on a former trip, we took a number of whistles. We also took some red calico, which one traveller on the mountain had declared to be invaluable in the mist. It could be torn into small strips and laid down to mark the trail. We didn't, however, make much use of it, and finally gave it away to one of the porters for his wife.

Fort Portal is the nearest town to the mountain, and here is situated the famous 'Mountains of the Moon' hotel, whose telegraphic address is just 'Romance'. In spite of numerous advertisements describing it as 'midst tropical snows', there was still a long way to go. The mountain was invisible. Hotel keeping absorbs a large proportion of the very few Europeans in Uganda who are not Government officials or missionaries. There must be almost as many hotel keepers as farmers, and it is probably a more profitable occupation. Some now combine hotel keeping with farming, using their old houses as the hotel, and carrying on the farm when they do not have too many guests to look after. Most of these hotels are fairly comfortable, but they cannot be called cheap. Still, one pays no more and no less for a night's lodging in the centre of Africa than one does at one of the best hotels in the centre of London.

Fort Portal was originally the seat of one of the early garrisons in Western Uganda, and the present headquarters of the Administration still stands on a little hill, and part is surrounded by a deep trench. The place was originally called Fort Gerry, but was renamed Fort Portal after one of the early administrators of Uganda. Now the fort is the centre of a medium sized town, and here are the best ducas (shops) in Western Uganda. Here we bought sweaters and blankets for our porters at the surprisingly low price of two shillings per garment. In Uganda a blanket is considered as a garment, since it is worn by day, knotted over the shoulders, as well as by night.

In this part of Toro, and among the volcanic foothills of Ruwenzori, there live a number of scattered farmers, growing coffee and now some tea. It is probably not a very profitable occupation, but the scenery is magnificent and the climate equable, in fact as good as anywhere in Uganda. The average temperature, we were told, varied only between 62 degrees Fahrenheit and 65 degrees Fahrenheit throughout the year. Since Fort Portal is over 5,000 feet above sea level it is rarely over hot. The vegetation around is luxuriant and the soil in many places must be good.

At Kampala we had first heard of Captain Chapman as a farmer who lived a lonely life in the foothills of Ruwenzori, near the base of the Nyamgasani river, and it had been suggested to us that we should try to enlist his help in managing a base camp for us at his farm. At Fort Portal we heard a little more about him, although not much. He still remained a rather mysterious figure. We were told that he had built a road of his own twenty-five miles from the main road almost up to his farm, but no one seemed to know exactly where this road started from or much about it. There was practically no traffic along it. There was also a rest camp near its head where we hoped to collect our porters.

The first night was spent at Nyakasura School, where we arrived after dark with a frantically boiling engine. This is a big school managed by Commander Callwall and Mr. Shillito under the Church Missionary Society. The school takes Africans of public school age. Some are sent on to the big college at Makerere, Kampala, but the majority finish with school here. Mr. Shillito told us something of his schemes for teaching nature study and observation among the boys, and I gathered that he was very successful at it. Such teaching is undoubtedly most important in Africa, where plant and animal life play a much larger part in everyday life than they do in urbanized England.

Football, above all other European games, has penetrated Africa deepest. At Nyakasura we saw the boys playing with great gusto. Cricket is much more rarely seen. Perhaps the physical frenzy of football takes the place in some small way, not only of their old tribal dances, which are now rather rare, but also of their minor wars and raids, which are almost extinct now in Uganda, except, perhaps, up in the north by the Abyssinian border. African games were not much in evidence, although there are several known. The favourite one is played with red seeds about the size of peas and a simple board marked into compartments, but the actual game is of a length and complexity rivalling even the Chinese Ma-Jong.

Somerville was thrilled by some clay modelling of small pots and figures which some of the boys had made, and we wished that we could have stayed longer to see some of them at work. Although bound much by traditional forms, these pots seemed to display in many cases an instinctive sense of form and decorative design, a feature which is probably still inherent in many Africans, especially those who have not come too much under the influence of European representational work.

Next morning the road was dead straight, a fine contrast to the other one, which had been nothing but a continual curl. This road runs from Fort Portal along all the eastern side of Ruwenzori before branching, one side for Katwe, the famous salt lake and the Congo border, the other for Mbarara and so back to Kampala, a circular tour which many visitors now make. For one moment we were privileged in getting a glimpse of the snow peaks rising ethereally above the clouds, like mountains half dreamed in an ecstasy of semiconscious awakening. Then the mist closed over them and we saw the snows no more for some weeks.

One of the most exciting events of this day was the proud signpost, 'SLOW DOWN EQUATOR'; on one arm was inscribed 'Northern Hemisphere', on the other 'Southern Hemisphere'. We duly slowed down, but did not actually stop. I have since regretted that we did not stop and photograph so unique a signpost.

The night was spent at Kilembe. Somewhat to our surprise we found Edwards and Taylor still there. There had been insufficient flour to feed a large force of porters, and so they had split into two parties. Gibbins and Oliver had gone up first to cut a path while the other two collected plants and insects around Kilembe, and they said that they found no shortage of interesting things. In fact, the flora and fauna here was very much richer in numbers of species than higher up. They were staying for the time at one of the guest houses at Kilembe, a house which looked pleasantly like an old English farmhouse. Behind, the green hills of Ruwenzori rose steeply.

Here we collected our safari, very nearly loading up on to our lorry some of Edwards's precious store of flour which had been put on our side of the shed by mistake. We had at this time five boys in all. Kabanga was the chief of them, and was a most valuable loan from the Agricultural Department, for whom he collected a small share of spoils in the form of such rats and their fleas as he might be able to obtain towards their census of such beasts. He had been with us before and proved most useful, being nearly always cheerful and unflustered. He was one of the few Africans we met who was able to order the putting up of tents which did not fall down again, and so on. Cerasi came to look after Somerville and myself, and to help with the safari organization, which he had done before. Then Erimoni, the boy with the perpetual grin, came to cook for us, which he did with conspicuous skill in spite of the most meagre apparatus. His scones made out of cassava flour in an old petrol tin were a triumph. With Buxton came Bernardo, a great tall fellow who was very swift at catching the elusive locust, and we hoped would be equally good at catching other insects. All these four were Baganda boys, who came from the Kampala district around the northwestern shores of Lake Victoria. They could all speak a little English and proved a valuable means of communicating with the porters when our own Swahili failed. But sometimes even they could not understand, as Uganda is a land of very many different languages.

From Kilembe the road passed along a dry plain, sparsely covered with thorn scrub. We had been told that this country around Lake George was very rich in game, and hoped to see at least some elephants. We were, however, disappointed in this. All the game we saw was two large warthogs which ran across the road almost in front of the car. I was not able to see them very clearly, but I got an impression that they were most peculiar and unpleasant beasts, bristling with tusks and stiff hairs, and much higher on their front legs than on their back.

We searched in vain for the opening of Captain Chapman's road and ran on to Katwe, where Buxton bought a sack of salt for our porters. At Katwe is the famous salt lake. This is a most peculiar little round lake, separated from Lake Edward only by a narrow tongue of land. Yet its level is nearly a hundred feet below that of Lake Edward. From the road we looked down on it almost directly below us. All this part of the country has been riddled with volcanic action in the past, and apparently the salt lake at Katwe is an explosion crater blown through pre-existing deposits of volcanic ashes. The salt supply seems unceasing. It is chiefly the ordinary common salt, but mixed with it there is a very small proportion of soda and of Glauber's salt, which gives it a medicinal value. Some of the salt, probably the purest, is gathered in pans on the side, but the greatest supply is dredged and almost raked out of the water. The lake is shallow, and little figures can be seen wading through it, dragging masses of salt behind them. We were told that in some lights the lake appears deep red in colour and the figures appear to be wading in a bath of blood. We did not, however, see this effect.

Our sack cost, I think, two or three shillings. It was good, though unrefined, salt. We were told that the output was generally over 2,000 tons per year, and this is distributed over much of Uganda and into the Congo. It is administered by the native government of Toro.

The salt has been a prosperous industry for many ages. Only now, with the competition of European salt in tins, is there likely to be any decline. We had already passed on the road lines of men carrying enormous long sausage-shaped bundles, bound up in banana fibre and slung between a framework of sticks. These they carried balanced on their heads. When they rested and stood their loads upright beside them, the bundles reached several feet above their heads. These bundles contained salt from the lake at Katwe. Many weighed two hundred pounds, but they carried them a considerable distance, sometimes, I believe, hundreds of miles.

Katwe is due south of the mountain, and now we had to turn north again. We followed the Indian lorry, which bore our equipment, along a small side road. This got rapidly worse and worse until we came to a bridge at which the Indian lorry driver jibbed. I rather agreed with him. So we unloaded the lorry and carried the stuff across the river. The bridge seemed to be made chiefly of matting and wattles suspended from a rather ancient wooden framework. I disembarked from Boanerges, our ancient car, such weight as was live weight, and then drove very slowly and cautiously across. Somerville said that the bridge sagged very visibly.

Still it was better than the next place, where there was no bridge at all, but a ford with a vertical bank two feet high on the other side and a drop in the stream just below. This we declined, and gathering as many porters as possible, sent forward the loads, while we went back for more from the lorry. It is wonderful how Africans always seem to appear out of an apparently deserted landscape. Soon we had gathered between forty and fifty. Somerville reported the same thing wherever he began to paint.

Once the heavy Boanerges went through a hidden bridge over a small trickle, lurching down on one back wheel. For half an hour we toiled feverishly with jacks and pieces of wood, but all with no avail. We pushed first forwards, then tried backwards. Just as we had made up our minds to leave the car, Buxton, with his old Ford, came along and towed us out unconcernedly.

As night fell we left the cars, pursuing our journey on foot to one of those delightful litttle rest camps which the beneficent local government of Uganda has sprinkled so freely over the country. There was a second one to receive us the next day, and above that only Ruwenzori, except for the lonely and very beautiful farm where Captain Paul Chapman lives surrounded by mountains and within sound of the incessant music of the Nyam-gasani river. Here we found him, and he readily undertook the job of running a base camp for us, sending up food to us in relays as we sent down porters loaded with specimens. Most nobly he did this, so that neither our porters nor ourselves were ever short of food the whole time. There is no food to be gained in the higher zones, and we were in perpetual fear that the supply would run out before the relays arrived, and that the porters would then leave us and our collections high upon the mountain, running down for food. Indeed, we could hardly have blamed them if they had done so.

This enabled us to extend our stay on the mountain considerably. Previously Chapman had managed parties of big-game hunters in Kenya, and so he knew what was wanted. In his garden all manner of fruit and flowers grew luxuriantly. Luckily he had grown a very fine crop of potatoes that year, and we were able to buy from him loads of these, and also some cassava and maize flour. We found that these were quite popular among the porters. So were the beans, of which we managed to obtain some loads grown locally. Chapman was also able to obtain some meat for us at intervals, which pleased the porters so much that they always over-ate to an astounding extent the night the meat arrived.

Chapman told us that the forest above was very thick and that we would have to cut a path all the way. He had never been up himself because of this difficulty. He suggested also that we needed some more pangas for cutting, and a few other extras. So I went back to the car and drove to Fort Portal for one night, an unexpected return to civilization after I felt we had abandoned it for at least a month. On my return I used Chapman's road. Quickly in Africa a road gets overgrown although it may be hard underneath. This was the oddest road we had yet travelled. Again we had difficulty in finding the place where it started, and had to go and ask at a neighbouring hut. Then we crossed a low sand ditch from the main road and drove off into the bush, leaving a fine pattern of arrows in the sand to guide Buxton, who was coming after. For twenty miles two thin tracks, and much faith, guided us through the tall grass. In front of us it rose unbroken until we mowed it down like a scythe. Behind us it rose again. Still the road was there below the vegetation, and after several hours we emerged on to the top of a hill, only a little above the rest camp. Here we left the car conveniently turned at the top of a steep hill, so that we might get a good run downhill to assist us in starting again on our return from the mountain. Bitter experience had taught us to think of such things.

Chapman had a logging camp a little further up, and there we moved next day, crossing on the way the rickety bridge shown in the photograph, a bridge which must often have been carried away when the river flooded. But still, it would be easily replaced: just a few poles and some brushwood tied together. Now the river was low. Above that we climbed a hill covered with tall elephant grass, the grass which is as tall as a man. We emerged on to a hilltop where was Chapman's highest hut, where he lived while he was getting wood from the forest. It

was a fine big hut built round a great tree. Unfortunately
there was neither window nor chimney, but still a certain
amount of light penetrated and we soon got used to the
smoke. It was medieval and primitive, but yet delightfully Rembrandt in the depths of its brown shadows
and its richness. Outside was a little experimental field
of wheat.

Here we enlisted more porters, since many of the
men from the camps below did not want to come further,
nor did we much want them. Chapman helped us and
sent out word for some of the mountain men whom he
knew. These were the real hardy spirits, men who
retired into the mountains whenever the local chief came
from below to collect such tiresome things as taxes. The
Congo border was only a few miles away and there was a
mountain path.

Funds were strictly limited in amount, so we had to
restrict ourselves to forty porters, although we could
have obtained and employed more. They were Bakonjo,
pleasant and friendly fellows, but much less civilized
than the majority of the Uganda peoples, who have had
considerable contact with European civilization. They
are an ancient race, since they have been little affected
by the Hamitic waves from the north and north-east,
merely retiring before them, like the Celts, to the mountains, where they have preserved their old language and
their powerful, heavy negroid stature and appearance.
We had two headmen, or Nyamparas, one to stay with
us and look after the porters and cutters, the other to
convoy relays up and down the mountain. The first was
an excellent fellow; he remained with us all the time and
became a friend. The second we hardly saw, but his old
red fez always betokened the arrival of more food, and
was consequently well received in the camp.

The Africans do not like the mountain, and hardly ever
climb it of their own accord. We were told that a large

safari of Bakonjo had ascended some distance about twelve years before in search of hyrax, and one man reported that he had seen the lakes in the distance, otherwise no one had been up. They fear the spirits of the mountain and hate its cold. Owing to the bad reputation of the range and the hard time experienced by porters in other valleys on some former expeditions, it is necessary to give a high wage. We paid one shilling a day per man to all those who went into or above the bamboo zone. On this we lost slightly, since the bamboos began nearly a thousand feet lower than we had anticipated. Each man was given a blanket and a sweater, brightly coloured, although not quite so thick as I would have liked. Still, I soon gathered that the bright colour was a greater recommendation than any thickness would have been. When we reached the higher zones each man was given one extra garment. The empty sacks were also used and made most excellent tunics, when holes were cut for head and arms. They were very popular.

The biggest lake had been marked by Humphreys opposite Mt. Watamagufu, the name which means 'The Strong Man'. There were three peaks visible up the valley from Chapman's camp, and he told us that he thought one of these was Watamagufu. Long we looked up the valley trying to anticipate a way.

There are many picturesque African names for the lower peaks and for the camps and rock shelters on the Mubuku route, although there seem to be no African names for the actual high peaks. This is sad, since many have been given rather incongruous names after worthy people of all nationalities. The peak at the head of the Nyamgasani was called Weismann peak after the famous German biologist, although he had no connection with Ruwenzori, or even with Africa as far as I know. One of the camps on the normal route is called Nyinitaba, which Humphreys told me meant 'Mother of Mud', a most appropriate name from his description of the conditions there.

Stanley, on his journey by the mountain in 1888, reported that the Africans with him had no conception of snow or its connection with water. They believed, somewhat naturally, that the white substance up on the mountain was salt.

For days we seemed to have packed and bargained. We were glad at last to leave behind us the heat and the perpetual elephant grass of the plains and foothills. These were curious little conical hills with steep sides. Somerville declared that to him they vividly suggested elephants, sitting down and sliding, rather out of control, into a sea below. Above us lay the forest, dark, mysterious, and all new ground.

CHAPTER II

THE RAIN MAN OF RUWENZORI

We set off to the accompaniment of a slow, haunting drum, which beat several days and several nights for an old man who had just died. We were told that he had been struck by lightning. What an omen and what a farewell sound! The slow, steady rhythm of Africa, so sure and so unhurrying, yet so passionate.

It was all unknown ground. There was no track. We had to cut a path all the way. We soon got used to the routine. We cut generally for two or three days; then all the porters were massed for moving camp. The next day we started cutting again. One of us, generally Buxton, who knew more of the native languages than Somerville or myself, would go ahead with the porters. Somerville would draw or shoot, while I would gather plants and take photographs, generally returning laden, and easily last, to camp. The cutters required almost continuous encouragement, although they actually decided the path under the guidance of an old man, who said that he had seen the lakes in the distance many years before when a party of Bakonjo had ascended the mountain to hunt hyrax. No one had been up since. The path he chose seemed good, although it made a considerable detour to avoid passing up the actual Nyamgasani river, which would probably have been the shortest route, but not nearly such an interesting one. We learnt later that the Bakonjo had some strange instinctive fear of the main river.

On some of the lower ridges there is bracken. Everywhere, or very nearly everywhere, in the world there is bracken. Here the cutting was easy. The first day I found the cutters making a road wide enough for a large car instead of the narrow track we wanted. They were still within sight of home. At intervals they would sit down, light a fire and smoke their picturesque pipes, made from banana petioles and three feet long. There was generally only one pipe among each group. Each man would take a long draw, completely filling his lungs, and then pass it on to the next man. The bowl was made from any large leaf which they could find, rolled round like a funnel and pushed into a small hole at the end of the pipe. The tobacco was also generally picked up by the wayside, but most of them seemed to look out for some particular leaves. Fire was generally carried in a smouldering bundle of bamboos. Whenever they stopped for a moment or two they would light a small fire and squat down round it. Often they would fail to put out the fire when they left, which was dangerous. Each man carried a tobacco pouch and bag, made from the whole skin of a hyrax or a monkey just sewn up down the side. Often inside the bag the dry stomach of the animal formed a pocket in which a knife could be kept. These were proud and cherished possessions. Some of them were very fine skins and had probably been handed down from father to son.

Among them we had one real wild man of the mountains, and he proved a great character. He had a magic whistle, a metal tube wrapped round with banana leaves. A few blasts from the whistle would keep the rain away. Every morning he would blow it and the clouds would pass. If, perchance, a few drops actually fell, his blasts would become more and more frantic; once when we had a short hailstorm he almost burst. An uncanny success seemed to attend his efforts. At his blasts even big black clouds were blown away, and we ourselves almost began to believe in the power of the whistle, while among the Africans his prestige must have become enormous. Probably they paid him a fraction of their wages to keep the weather fine for them. He was also much more familiar with the mountain than the others, being able to find his way through the forest and to snare the rock hyrax. He seemed to delight in the mountain in a way that none of the others did. Something of its superb wildness and loneliness had entered into his soul.

We were unable to find out much about the whistle and the ideas underlying its use. He had not made it himself, but had bought it some time previously from a witch doctor for two goats. The power seemed to reside rather in the whistle than in the man, since before the end of the expedition he fell slightly ill and had to leave us. He passed on the whistle to another man, and apparently the results were the same, although his skill in blowing it was not nearly so great. The mountain positively beamed on us. After a few days in which there was some mist and rain, we had almost continuous fine weather and long sunny days. We met no snow except that which already lay on the ground, and only one real hailstorm. How far this wonderful weather was due to our wild man with the whistle, and how far to the dry season below, I would rather leave to my readers. It would be pleasant to think that his great faith was effective in at least some small part.

Soon we emerged from the bracken into the forest. Like all transitions of vegetation on Ruwenzori, it was abrupt. The forest covered all the ridges above 6,500 feet and stretched great tongues down the valleys beside the rivers. It was not such a gloomy place as some forests I have seen. In frequent patches a Melastomaceous tree with clusters of large pink flowers, flowers not unlike small single roses, interrupted the continuous green. Few could fail to be thrilled by the giant tree ferns and the wild bananas, some of the most graceful and beautiful of plants. Surely foliage is just as important from the point of view of decoration, as flower. These plants gave dignity and distinction to the undergrowth. Although small beside the gigantic specimens of New Zealand, some of the tree ferns were fifteen feet in height. They had enormous fronds emerging from a stem, slender and often charmingly curved, yet so prickly as to repel most painfully any close contact.

The wild bananas bore no fruit, but had hard seed like large rounded beans which germinated freely. This is the only banana, as far as I know, which can be grown from seed. We have them growing in England from this seed, and already their leaves are six feet high after eighteen months. One friend brutally described them as the bananas which 'have never done anything about it', referring to their absence of edible fruit. If, however, we consider their biological purpose as growing and repro-ducing, the other bananas with fruit but no seed would rather merit this description. The vast leaves of bright emerald green were edged with pale pink through which the sunlight penetrated in a translucent glimmer. The midrib also was pink. I know no leaves through which sunlight penetrates more beautifully than those of the banana. Every vein was delineated like the barbs of a fine quill feather or the crests of the waves of the sea. To stand underneath them and look up at the sun pro-vided a real thrill. The leaves were largely untorn, and did not present the tattered appearance of the common banana. Although often ten or more feet in height, the plants were practically trunkless, the leaves arising from a great cradle formed by the old leaf bases, to which age had imparted a deep crimson colour. Beside the small plant presses these leaves indeed presented a botanist's dilemma. We found many such dilemmas on the mountain.

A group of these wild bananas grew beside a delightful little stream, and at the ford the sunlight penetrated and lit up the outstretched fronds of the tree ferns and the big leaves of the wild bananas with peculiar brilliance.

At the edge of the stream grew a very beautiful pink balsam. Luckily, all the rivers were low and we were easily able to reach this plant. Its flowers seemed to float on the end of slender red stems like delicate shell-pink butterflies with wings outspread. It was certainly one of the most attractive balsams I have ever seen. This plant I have introduced to England, and in a cool green-house it has flowered continuously for a whole year. We hadn't yet reached the zones of frost, and so the plants here cannot be absolutely hardy in England. The growth everywhere was very luxuriant; the trees were covered with tangled lianas, festooned with streamers of liver-worts and tussocked with moss. This was, indeed, a place in which to stand and ponder, one of those rare corners which seem outside the ordinary busy world, a place where the clock stands still and perfect inward peace blends with an outer peace. Such places and moods are rare. This one will be a memory to us for long.

Here we first saw the Colobus monkey, which is common on Ruwenzori. It is a magnificent beast, and from close up looks like an old man with its superb white whiskers and face framed with white fringe. Behind hangs down a long white tail. A herd of them crashing through the branches is a wonderful spectacle. We also saw the rarer blue monkey, a big grey beast which appears to be solitary in its habits. Once, when collecting alone, I spent several minutes watching an unusually large one, which sat on a branch only a few yards away and delicately devoured a fruit. After every bite he would look up at me and shake his head as if to say, 'All right, Gov'nor', almost smiling with a cockney impudence. Finally he finished the fruit, threw the skin in my direction and vanished into the forest.

A forest of vast bamboos formed the next zone. Above us the feathery spikes formed arches over our camp, and the tall straight stems helped the feeling that we were in some very ancient cathedral. Only a dim and fitful light penetrated. Our camp fires made from dead bamboos flickered like small candles against the overpowering atmosphere of the forest, and a very real forest these bamboos formed. It was a curious green world: the roof was green, the stems of the bamboos were green, the ground was covered with ferns and mosses in innumerable shades of green. Only an occasional dead and leaning bamboo gave a touch of purple or brown. On the bamboo stems were huge purple slugs.

Although we had cleared quite a large space for the camp, before we left the bamboos had arched again over us, so flexible are their stems. Below them our men flitted silently about like shades and shadows from the underworld. There was little sound, only a rustle of the leaflets, a soft murmuring in the wind and an occasional ghostly creaking and cracking as of some spirit laughing at us. This almost enchanted world seemed to have a deadening and depressing effect on the camp. Few men sang or shouted or laughed. They ate their food in silence, whispering in muffled tones. Through the forest bats flitted silently—bats in the bamboos.

We cut down and measured two of the finest bamboos around our camp; they were both over fifty feet in length and eleven inches in circumference at the base. These seemed a record to us at the time, but in the Natural History Museum I have since seen a bamboo from Burma over eighty feet. In many of the older stems were small holes, out of which we collected mosquito larvæ, which breed in the accumulated water of the hollow stems. These were Kabanga's job. He kept the larvæ and pupæ in old jam jars, and managed to breed out a few very interesting mosquitoes. When we moved camp he carried these jars himself most carefully in a little bag with two handles, exactly like a little boy who had been gathering tiddlers.

The forest also had a depressing effect on the porters. One morning, early, we heard murmurings throughout the camp. When I emerged from my tent I was not surprised to see a little line of men waiting there.

At the camp here a few men had thought that it would be a suitable time to attempt a strike. And came demanding larger wages and clothing, although it was not yet cold and the work was not very strenuous. The loads were kept down to thirty pounds, although the usual rate in East Africa is forty-five or fifty. But in many places on Ruwenzori the ground was very difficult for porters. Captain Chapman had remained below, and they saw in us three youngsters who they no doubt thought would be easy game. The majority of Africans, somewhat naturally, regard the Englishman's money as inexhaustible: if he runs out he has only to send a piece of paper to the bank and they send along a fresh supply. They are also extremely faithful to one another, and although ninety-nine men out of a hundred are contented, they will nearly always support the one agitator, even if it means giving up a good job for it.

Although such minor troubles occasionally occurred and had to be suppressed, whenever I thought over the past few hours I felt that they were always the result of some slight impatience or perhaps unconscious unreasonableness on our part: that we, rather than they, were to blame. The depressing effect of the forest needed to be counteracted by extra kindness and cheerfulness on our part. Here, perhaps, a portable gramophone would have been useful. The African is seldom either illogical or alogical in his thoughts or actions.

I had momentary fears of the expedition collapsing at the start, since any increase in the wages was out of the question. They were already getting a shilling a day per man, which is great wealth for an African peasant. On the six weeks' work they did for us they would be able to pay their poll tax and probably live for the rest of the year in comfort; it would even admit of quite a good beer supply, and practically all the Uganda natives we met were much addicted to the consumption of this banana beer.

Their agitation, however, soon subsided when they realized that they either accepted their pay or went, leaving behind the blankets and sweaters which had been issued to them. When two or three had been mercilessly stripped of their extra clothing, which in most cases formed almost their entire wardrobe, there was little more trouble. A very few faint-hearted ones left, and Captain Chapman soon replaced these for us, while the remainder cheerfully shouldered their loads, laughing and singing as usual. 'Clop, clop, crack' went the cutters, and the bamboos quickly fell before their pangas, leaving villainous spikes a foot from the ground. Bamboo Camp was pitched close to a large rock shelter, under which some of the porters slept. For the most part they seemed to prefer the outer fly which they had erected on a framework of bamboos as a shelter, and under which they had made a fire. Here they would heat large pots of flour mixed with water into a kind of dough. Each man would dip out of the pot with his fingers, squatting round the fire.

These rock shelters consist of large overhanging rocks and have been used by all former explorers to the mountain. They are apparently characteristic of Ruwenzori.

From the top of the rock shelter we were able to get a view up the valley. Otherwise our progress through the forest was blind. From this rock in the distance we caught our first glimpse of the snow, just a sprinkling, obviously fresh. The actual snow peaks were not visible. Though we had by now missed our chance of spending an old-fashioned Christmas up by the snow, we still hoped that we might get there by the New Year. However, to celebrate the first sight of snow we had a plum pudding preceded by curried bully beef. It is surprising how a little curry powder will transform that rather unappetising compound into quite a reasonable dish, entirely disguising its origin. So strong was the effect of this fine dinner on David Buxton—normally a vegetarian—that he proposed that from henceforward all meals should be discontinued until further notice. Any further food seemed, to him, unnecessary for a long time. The motion was, however, rejected.

Although the weather was good, the forest seemed always damp and muddy. The tussocks of moss and liverwort still held the water like a sponge. Only on the way down, after more than a month of fine weather, did we notice any perceptible drying up of the forest. The path was generally steep and quickly became very slippery. We slithered on through the inevitable mud up and down innumerable ravines, at the bottom of which were small streams—tributaries of the Nyamgasani. Immediately around the streams the bamboo forest changed and other trees grew. Often they were festooned, like fairy bowers, with moss and liverwort, and made bright with the scarlet *Choananthus*, a superb Amaryllid with a mop-like head of drooping bell-shaped flowers. There was also a wicked-looking *Arisæma*, the snake lily, spotted brown, green and white. It was all very unreal. During our time on Ruwenzori the feeling was very strongly with us that our adventure was merely a dream, and that we should suddenly wake up to find ourselves back in the more ordinary and more materialistic world.

'Burnt Tree' Camp was our next. It was pitched at the foot of a large *Podocarpus* tree at 9,000 feet. The base of the trunk was blackened, and it was obvious that a fire had been made there before—probably by some wandering party of Bakonjo. It made an excellent fireplace, although it seemed rather sacrilege to treat in this way such a magnificent tree. Looking upwards into the branches lit up from below with the golden light of the fire, we were reminded of the exquisite decoration of some stage fantasy or mysterious ballet. With the light below, the streaming lichens and the feathery foliage seemed golden-red and artificial. All the land here sloped steeply, and we had some trouble in finding and then enlarging enough flat ground for the tent. Even then 'Burnt Tree' was a camp in tiers. Somerville went out with the rain man, looking for wild pig, which he said were to be found near here, but was unsuccessful. There were no paths, but this man seemed to have an uncanny, an almost animal, sense of direction, a gift now lost to most civilized peoples. Sometimes he would stop, look around on to the ground and up into the trees, almost sniff the air like a dog; then suddenly he would decide the direction and the party would move off again. Near the camp we found a large, but long disused, wooden trap which we were told had been designed to catch the large forest hog. But none had used it for many years.

Here I fell ill with an attack of malaria, but was up and about again in two days, while David Buxton went on and pitched the next camp.

Gradually the bamboos diminished in size, dwindling from fifty feet to fifteen, until suddenly we emerged into a zone of tree heathers. Imagine a haunted wood composed of ordinary ling heather magnified fifty times; there were trees fifty feet high instead of bushes of one foot, twisted into weird shapes and gnarled so that each resembled a drawing by Arthur Rackham. Out of each trunk glared a face, sometimes benign, more often wicked and bearded with streamers of lichens and mosses.

Looking out between the tree heathers we could see far into the mountain across a wide expanse of ridges and gorges, but there were no signs either of the lakes or the snowfields which we had hoped to see. It seemed a wild and desolate expanse, in very truth a place where no man lived or would be likely to live. It was not only bare, but mysterious and unearthly. There was no sound. Here the silence became the voice. When grey and misty it seemed to present a challenge to the man who invaded its solitude; the mountain appeared antagonistic to man and tried to frighten him back again with its uncanny aspect, its cold, its dampness, and the rather putrescent smell which arose from the *Mimulopsis*. This is a vigorous white-flowered plant covering the ground underneath the heathers with a five-foot thicket. Even from the highest branches dangled long sulphurous yellow strands of the Usnea lichen, the old man's beard of many travellers, which Somerville declared reminded him of the hair of Botticelli's angels, an extremely apt comparison in the sunlight. In the mist they resembled nothing so essentially happy, but appeared rather as some melancholy ghosts, not of the animal, but of the vegetable world, the lost souls of a past vegetable glory flapping their branches and stretching out to frighten the wretched man who dared to penetrate such places. It is, indeed, a place of mystery, haunting when these shapes stand out dimly from a background of swirling mists. Among these the stiff spikes of the lobelias barred our path like figures with upright lances. In present-day life such plants seem out of place: they are rather the complement of prehistoric man, or even the giant reptiles and pterodactyls.

When the sun shone, and it frequently did so for us, the aspect of the mountain changed very quickly and immediately became friendly. Everything then smiled at us; the pink and white everlasting flowers opened into a mass of colour, while the most gorgeous little blue sunbirds appeared and flitted among the lobelias, poking their long beaks into the blue flowers and climbing with agility round the great spikes. The male is indeed resplendent with glossy metallic feathers of brilliant turquoise and emerald, but the female is a dingy brown. They are the African equivalent of the humming bird.

We pitched our third camp at 11,000 feet and christened it Heather Ridge Camp, for it was on the divide between the Nyamgasani valley and the Congo Lume to the west. We could look down into both systems. The western side of the mountain has the reputation of being even wetter than the eastern, and during the few days we spent at this camp it was noticeable that the mist always filled the Lume valley before that of the Nyamgasani. Here we had our only hailstorm, and our rain man showed considerable agitation with his whistle. Bending forward, he looked up to the clouds, seemingly lost in a frenzy of asking.

Luckily the tents and porters' shelter had been erected, and the storm was only a short one, although very heavy. At this camp we received an extremely welcome mail, forwarded to us by Captain Chapman. Several of the letters had been written in England less than a fortnight before and sent out by air mail. While everything around was so strange, this seemed to bring us very near to England. Among mine was an excellent book about the Antarctic sent by a kind aunt as a Christmas present, and no doubt intended as an antidote to the heat of Uganda. Here, right on the equator, it was extremely cold.

We were by now exactly opposite the peak which Chapman had said was Watamagufu, although separated from it by the wide and deep Nyamgasani valley. There were no signs of any lakes. The Nyampara then told us that the mountain opposite was not Watamagufu; it was a mountain unmarked on the map. It was castellated and pinnacled with little peaks like a gothic building, but it was not Watamagufu, the mountain which meant 'Strong Man'. He pointed away into the distance and led us to believe that Watamagufu was beyond and behind the pinnacled mass opposite us.

29

Far below, David Buxton drew my attention to two long regular ridges, standing high up from the depths of the Nyamgasani valley and running parallel for a distance of several miles up and down the valley. These were evidently moraines left by the great Nyamgasani glacier, which must have descended this valley during one of the pluvial periods which represented the great Ice Age in tropical Africa. The moraines run down to about 9,000 feet, and the glacier must have remained at this level for a great length of time, since the moraines are of enormous size. For shorter periods it probably descended several thousand feet lower. Moraines have also been recorded from other valleys much below the present snow line. Once the icecap must have been far larger than at present. What a magnificent mountain Ruwenzori must then have been! Unfortunately, those were prehistoric times.

At night the valley resounded with gruesome shrieks and screeches, which seemed to herald the approach of some dreadful monster or the conversation of a party of prehistoric ghouls. They seemed so uncanny that I, at least, felt momentarily cold and shivery, until I remembered what a fearsome noise even the domestic cat can make at night. We found that they were made by the rock hyrax, small and very harmless beasts, superficially rather like rabbits, but by zoological systematists classified nearer to the elephant and the rhinoceros than to any other group. They are closely allied to the cony of the Bible. By day they live hidden and quiet among the rocks. On Kilimanjaro I believe they also are numerous, and are hunted for their fur, which is very soft. The people catch them in snares, and a young one was brought into us one morning by the rain man. I bought it from the hunter for fifty cents. No one else seemed able to catch them; they were quite unhurt. It was a delightful little beast. Both Somerville and my boy suggested that we should keep it as a pet, and somewhat weakly I gave way, although slightly unhappy in my scientific conscience, since we had been asked to collect skins of small mammals, and especially the fleas from such small mammals as we might get. Fortunately, next day we obtained an adult hyrax which was duly slain in the cause of science. There were no parasites. The young one lived for several days and soon became very tame, eating grass and other leaves and almost purring when it was stroked under the chin. It gave no signs of screeching at night, although it must have heard the noises around. Then one morning, on returning from collecting, I found a mournful camp, and was told that the young hyrax had suddenly died. Somerville and Kabanga were very sad; we could only think that it had eaten something which had not agreed with it. It seemed hard to believe that so much noise could be made by such small animals, but the Bakonjo all assured us that it was so, and on our return we looked up the Report of the former British Museum Expedition and found that they recorded the same noise and had identified it with the hyrax.

The next morning's march was full of plant thrills. A golden Sedum of positively gigantic size first attracted my attention as it sprawled luxuriantly over a large rock. The Heather forest became more and more like the haunted wood of the old fairy tale, and the carpet of evil Mimulopsis scrub gave place to a lower-growing Alchemilla, a plant with a silvery-green leaf and a burnt sienna stem. A tree St. John's Wort, *Hypericum Bequaertii*, next sent me into raptures. The flowers were nearly as large as tulips and hung delicately like orange lanterns from the ends of the branches. The sheer exuberance of the growth of the giant groundsels and the lobelias is astounding and thrilling. One rosette of *Lobelia Bequaertii* would often be several feet across, and would have several hundred closely-packed leaves, shining purple and radiating from the centre, where a drop of water would be enshrined like a jewel at the heart of the world. When this lobelia flowered it threw up a stiff green obelisk-like spike, monstrous and bizarre, but very much in keeping with the surroundings. I believe even the Monkey Puzzle looks well in its Chilean home, although there are varied opinions as to its desirability for small gardens in this country. The other dominating species was *Lobelia Wollastonii*, named after Dr. A. F. R. Wollaston, who visited the mountain in 1906. We had also found it on the Birunga mountains. Its spike is a glorious powder blue. When the sun touches the dewdrops on its blue flowers and grey bracts the whole spike seems touched with a silvery radiance. Against it the iridescent sunbirds look like emeralds and sapphires. The stem is pitted with a decoration of regular diamonds which makes even the dead plant interesting. There is nothing at present in English gardens to compare adequately with these lobelias. In superficial appearance, although nowhere in Systematics, the only plant I can mention is the noble Eremurus, but even this does not attain to the size of the lobelias.

It was just over 12,000 feet when we made our next camp by a small stream right among the lobelias and giant groundsels. Two lobelias formed our doorpost, and the tent ropes were tied to giant groundsels. The mosses were thicker here than anywhere else on the mountain. To sit down and rest was like reclining in a feather bed, brilliant not only with greens, but also with orange and crimson.

Above us the valley broadened out, forming a most delightful garden, full of flowers, framed with steep ridges on three sides. At the head were three rocky peaks, and between them two passes, one leading back presumably into the main valley of the Nyamgasani, and the other into that of the Lume. We hoped that from the top of this pass we would at last see the chain of lakes and the snows of Luigi. We had already been longer on the ascent than we had expected. This camp we named 'Speculation Camp', since we were all anxious as to what we might see in the morning from the top of the pass, and had indulged in many fanciful speculations. The next morning was bright and we made an early start. The cutters worked well, but the distance to the top of the pass proved longer than we had expected.

Somerville called the valley 'Paradise Valley'. It was walled like a natural garden, with grey hills covered with everlasting flowers, heathers and tree groundsels. It seemed different from the other parts of the valley. A fairy-like but very kindly spirit seemed to pervade it as the little blue sunbirds flitted in the sunlight. They were more numerous here than anywhere else on the mountain, and the air was full of their twittering-tweeting. Everywhere there were flowers, bushes of white and pink everlasting, powdery blue lobelia spikes, the purple of the *Lobelia Bequaertii*, and the golden of the tree groundsels, yet it was an orderly, not a tangled riot as on the rest of the mountain. It was like a place imagined in dreams. We were very happy as we rested there before breasting the steep slope up to the pass. Around us the porters shed their loads and lolled about in the grass and heather, chatting easily. These rests on the mountain march were some of our pleasantest times. By now they found little suitable material for smoking, and were delighted with the cigarettes which we distributed. When everyone had smoked a bit, the Nyampara and I would go round rousing them, 'Kwenda, Kwenda, tugende', lifting the loads back on to their heads.

This morning I went on with the Nyampara and the first cutters. As I looked down, I could see the loads rising almost vertically below me, so steep was the slope; but no one complained or dropped a load.

Here the tree heathers were replaced with a thick scrub of white everlasting flowers, through which it was extremely tiring to battle one's way. About ten o'clock we reached the top and saw, far away, the snows of Mt. Luigi di Savoia and a black lake at the foot of a towering dark mass—Mt. Watamagufu at last! Although very distant we could see the lake quite clearly. It was almost jet black and looked most mysterious; at the southern end was a small island of some pink rock. It was, however, too far away to reach in one march, and eventually it was another week before we had cut a path right through and carried all our camp there. We also climbed one of the peaks at the top of the valley to which our aneroid gave a height of 13,550 feet. No such high peaks had previously been recorded here.

'Rush Camp' we called our next. It was pitched beside a stream in an open patch covered with tussocks of the Ruwenzori carex, now fairly dry, but probably in wet weather a complete swamp. These rise about two feet from the ground like gigantic toadstools. In dry weather a tussock makes an excellent seat. In wet weather the channels between are full of water and travellers have to jump perilously from one wobbly tussock to the next. All around was a forest of tree heathers and giant groundsels, seemingly like an enchanted world, a botanist's nightmare, as the twisted trunks all writhed towards him. In the morning the sun shone on a dreamlike mist, which filled the valley and softened the peaks. In the foreground the lobelias and senecios seemed black, silhouetted against the radiant blue and soft grey of the mountains and the mist. Over the edge a cascade of white and pink everlastings fell into the depths of the valley. It was indeed a rare effect.

At last we reached the lake and stood at the top of another low pass and looked down on the black water, against which stood the spikes of two lobelias, dark, like acolytes holding up colossal candles. It looked a weird and mysterious place, and we gazed dreamily for a few moments until the spell was broken by voices behind us: 'Bakshish, Bwana, Bakshish.' It was an odious reminder of the advance of civilization, which we wanted at that moment to forget, nor had we thought such a word known to our rather uncivilized porters. I fear that they got no money, although that night they all got an extra ration of flour and beans and some meat to celebrate the success of the first part of the journey.

CHAPTER III

THE MOUNTAIN HITS BACK

THE next morning there was whispering in camp, and Kabanga came to say that the men did not want to go to a camp by the lake. They had communicated their fear also to him, so that he now vaguely feared the lake, although before he had never given it a thought, being superficially a typical product of Kampala sophistication. Still, this incident showed how superficial the influence of his mission education and of his training in the Government Laboratory really was. None of these men had ever been so high as the lakes. We soon learnt, though, that there was a tradition, a legend, associated with these lakes and that the local chief had reminded them of this before they had started. However, after a little discussion the fear seemed to blow away and we set out over the hillside and down a steep slope into a small valley. There was now only one ridge separating us from the lake. As Somerville and I came up I found them all sitting round at the foot of a big shelter, enjoying the usual rest. Then the head man came forward and said they wanted to camp here. We wanted to camp by the lake, since we had much work to do there.

We all sat down under the big rock shelter, well out of sight of the lake, and discussed the matter. They were afraid to go near the lakes or to drink out of them, and affirmed that it meant death to do so. They were equally afraid for us to go near, since they did not want us to die. The latter point they explained with great charm. Lower down, many of the tribes have a legend associated with the small volcanic lakes. In the past, a tribe of super men came out of these lakes and later returned down under the water. The present people have a taboo against drinking water from these. The Nyamgasani lakes were obviously not volcanic, but glacial; still it is possible that they were thinking of this legend.

Finally, we decided to pitch a camp on a small hillock about two hundred yards from the middle of the seventh lake. It was arranged that the porters should return for the first night to the last camp and bring up more loads. After that we gave them permission to sleep under the large rock shelter the other side of the last pass and just out of sight of the lake, coming up to us every morning.

However, after a little time they appeared to conquer their fear, and came up of their own accord to sleep at our camp, when they saw that we still survived. Opinion swayed round to our side, and I even heard a few murmurs that the chief was a foolish old man, babbling of matters of which he had no personal experience.

They would not take any water from the lake, but took it always from a small trickle which flowed through a Carex bog into the lake close to our camp. Once down by the lake I felt thirsty and drank a little water out of it, suffering no ill-effects. We took water samples for analysis both from this lake and from the one above, which appeared to be the chief centre of the fear. This one lay in the middle of a large marsh and did not look nearly so healthy as the one by which we were encamped. Unfortunately, the bottles got broken on the way down, so there is no chance of finding out whether there was any chemical foundation for their theories. There was another rock shelter just down by the lake, but it was not so big as the one under which we had held our discussion, which could easily have sheltered thirty or forty men. Some large animal had obviously been using it. Buxton was particularly interested and tried digging in the dust beneath it, in the hopes of finding bones or worked flints, but we found nothing of particular interest.

These rock shelters are very characteristic of Ruwenzori. They are great masses of rock thrown or squeezed up at a time of geological activity and faulting, and left sloping outwards.

By mid-day Somerville and I had established our camp by the lake; Buxton had remained at Rush Camp and intended to come up the next day with the remainder of the loads. We were still uncertain whether this was the seventh or the eighth lake recorded by Dr. Humphreys. No further lakes could be seen from our camp. I suspected, though, that it was the seventh; so after lunch Somerville and I started out to explore southwards to search for another lake. The vegetation round the lake was very thick, and we scrambled up and down ridges, sometimes having to battle our way through thick scrub. It seemed impossible to keep right down by the lake, so we climbed upwards on to the ridges, hoping always to get a clear view. At last we did, and saw below us yet another lake, almost as large as the one by which we were encamped. This eighth lake was distinguished by great sinuous masses of green weed which spread out far into the water.

Although their vegetation gave the lakes a weird and mysterious appearance, they had something in common with the Highland loch, while the Nyamgasani resembled some fast-flowing Highland river with pools of brown water. Our thoughts turned naturally to salmon and trout, and it seemed likely that these lakes would make an excellent home for trout. No one could ever hope to fish in more beautiful surroundings.

On one side rose the towering black mass of Mt. Watamagufu; at the head of the valley could be seen the snow ridge of Mt. Luigi, while the banks were clothed with tree heathers, everlastings, lobelias and giant groundsels. In our scrambling round the lake we came on one of the most perfect spots that I have ever seen.

The lake narrowed between cliffs which gleamed pink in the evening light, before flowing in a series of miniature waterfalls down to the eighth. Beside it was a small strip of brilliant green rush, which on Ruwenzori takes the place of grass. A beautifully pink tree heather, twisting snake-like, was mirrored in the black water, while beside it rose a mighty blue lobelia spike. Below these, rushes hung over into the water in graceful curves. Behind rose the hillside dark with giant heather and groundsels. A little pink island crowned with a lobelia spike was reflected in the water down to every detail, as in some fairy scene portrayed in a black mirror. Behind the little island the lake widened, seeming to end in a medley of rocks crowned by the snows of Luigi. On either side the cliffs framed the scene. Somerville drew for a while, while I rested on the rushes and gazed either into the water or up into the sky, marvelling at this symphony of colour. Perfect peace reigned.

The water was mysteriously dark, but every now and then the rays of the setting sun would send glorious golden streaks across it. I have only seen one lake to compare with it: Lake Louise, which is set like a blue jewel at the foot of a glacier in the Canadian Rockies and is framed with dark pine woods.

While we were there the surface temperature of the water never went below 40 degrees Fahrenheit, although ground temperatures below freezing were recorded from our camp, and in the morning we often found ice on our washing basins. We were unable to find any trace of fish, and it seems hard to see how they could have got there unless artificially introduced. I do not know of any indigenous cold-water fish recorded from East Africa. There appeared ample fish food: great numbers of small bivalve molluscs were floating on the surface, while there were caddis fly larvæ and plenty of algal and other water weeds. Trout have been introduced successfully into several East African mountain streams, but never as high as this. From the edge also we got a sample of plankton, but were unable to obtain any from the centre. The possibility of making a raft out of Senecio wood, which has a thick cork layer, was discussed, but we did not have time to carry the project out, and so the complete biological exploration of the lake still remains for a future expedition.

We found some duck and were able to secure a pair. It was identified as *Anas sparsa*, the black-headed duck, a species widespread in the higher regions of Africa. Fragments of broken egg-shell indicated that they were breeding up there. Duck shooting and trout fishing, together with rock climbing and a little glacier work, would make it a wonderful playground if only the mountain did not have such an evil reputation for weather!

While Somerville drew I explored alone up the valley and passed three more lakes. The valley was full of little hillocks and rose irregularly. The top of each proved a spur to the imagination and taunted me so that finally I went much further than I had intended and had to run back to camp to get in before dark and appease the anxiety of my companions. These three lakes seemed of a different character to the lower two. Buxton suggested that they were formed originally behind dams of morainic material left by the retreating glacier. Now, however, they are bounded by sedgy swamp land, which is gradually encroaching on them, and has in places completely roofed over the meandering streams which join the lakes. The two lower lakes, confined in a narrow valley, seem to be rock basins scooped by the ice of the glacier when it extended far down the valley. Their outflows pass over solid rock.

Opposite the sixth lake I saw a peak, shaped like a plum cake. This was obviously the Keki peak, so named by Dr. Humphreys, who said that its shape had particularly impressed itself on their minds owing to their hunger at the time. From the marsh beside this lake rose a beautiful snipe; we were never able to secure a specimen, so its exact identity still remains veiled.

In the evening we all sat round a large wood fire outside the tent. It was one of the great features of the trip. Surely no other expedition on Ruwenzori has had such luck. Generally we read of them cowering in tents or under rock shelters while the rain poured down outside. Round the fire the bundles of plants stood erect and became gradually dry. Sometimes I felt almost like an old washerwoman carefully tending and drying her clothes; only they received much more care than I am sure any laundry gives. Wood from the giant groundsel burnt with a rather suffocating smoke, but the giant heather and bamboo made good fuel. When in Borneo we had a gramophone, which played in the evening and kept the Borneans very happy around the camp, helping especially to break down the distance between them and us. I felt that a gramophone here would have been an advantage for that reason and worth the extra porter, although we ourselves were obviously very happy without it. Our only controversy was a very slight one. It concerned a fine Dutch cheese, scarlet outside and round like a football. It came out of a tin. But none of us had ever tasted a Dutch cheese like it before. It was absolutely unique in its flavour and had a taste of the finest Rochefort about it. Whether long incarceration in the tin, or the effect of being jolted up the mountain on a man's head, was responsible for this we could not tell. We could only wonder at it. Now Buxton was very fond of macaroni cheese, and advocated cooking it for this together with baked beans, which made an excellent dish. Somerville and I said that it was much too fine a cheese for that fate. However, we compromised by cutting it in half.

There were many tracks about the mountain, which showed the presence of small mammals, but we never actually saw any. Once up by the sixth lake, while the porters were resting, a sudden cry arose and several of them started to their feet and ran, whooping with delight, to some rocks fifty yards off. But when they got there they found nothing. Somerville said that he had seen a small black animal, just disappearing into a hole by the rocks. I had, unfortunately, missed it. Perhaps it was a new race of black hyrax. We heard the hyrax very clearly at night and several were caught. Somerville once reported hearing a loud and mysterious bark in the undergrowth near him, but saw nothing; on Mt. Dulit, in Sarawak, we had had a mythical animal called an Igok, which ate men, leaving only the hat. We never saw one. Perhaps this Ruwenzori bark belonged to the same category. There is known a Ruwenzori duiker, a small species of antelope. Tracks of leopard are also reported to have been seen up by the snows. The scarcity of rats was very pronounced. Kabanga was not able to catch any in his traps. One evening, when we were sitting in the tent, Somerville suddenly exclaimed, 'Look there', and stretched out his hand to the tent wall. He brought it back with a small rat held firmly by the tail. After that we chaffed poor Kabanga to further efforts, saying, 'If the Bwana can catch a rat with his hands, why can't you catch any with all your traps?' However, he never succeeded. Stupendous chameleons with three horns had been recorded from Ruwenzori. We were most anxious to obtain some, but were unsuccessful, in spite of offering as a last resort large financial rewards to anyone who could bring one in. Birds were frequent, although not very varied. There was a large black-and-white crow which circled high over our camp. Among the rocks were numbers of swifts and also flocks of a bird rather like small starlings. There were duck on the lake. The little sunbirds flitting among the lobelias were perfect jewels.

We decided to pitch a small camp, just one tent by the fourth lake recorded by Humphreys, and from there to make an attempt on the Weismann peak, the highest point of Mount Luigi di Savoia. The snow peak was completely hidden by the rocky mass which towered above us at the end of the valley. Our objective was eclipsed, and in a weak moment we named our camp 'Eclipse' Camp, a name truly prophetic of its destiny.

Camp was made soon after midday, and two of us started out to prospect a route, leaving the third alone to prepare tea against our return. We had sent back the porters and boys who had helped us to pitch camp, since we were anxious not to expose them to more cold than necessary, and no one of them was equipped for snow or ice. Also we felt a desire to be alone on the mountains for at least a day or two, and away from the bustle of the bigger camp.

On this afternoon we reached the lowest snow patches, and found a route to the peak which appeared to be possible. We also saw Dr. Humphreys' third lake, a glacial basin situated below a steep rock face at 14,350 feet. In colour it was deep green, very rich and very mysterious. It was smaller than the lower lakes, but yet it must have been two hundred yards long and fifty wide.

At this height the vegetation was very sparse, and consisted chiefly of a black, rather dried-up lichen which covered the sloping rocks and made them very slippery. There were occasional small bushes of a very woolly everlasting, while in pockets there were some low grasses and mosses. We also found a very few small Senecio plants as high as 14,600 feet, just at the foot of the glacier. Instead of the rich vegetation of below, these barren rocks called to mind rather some lunar landscape. An interesting discovery in this zone was the daddy

43

longlegs, whose females were short winged and crawled over the rocks, unable to fly. We also found some pink worms in ponds left by the snow. There were also short-winged females of a small carpet moth, and some very tiny flies completely devoid of wings.

We looked down from here to the valley below and were surprised to see a small cloud round our camp which bore a remarkable resemblance to smoke. Such large fires were absolutely unrecorded from Ruwenzori, and it seemed scarcely possible.

On our way down we looked again and decided that it really was smoke. Our camp was completely hidden by the cloud, which now filled the whole valley between the fourth and the fifth lakes. We hurried on down as fast as possible, fearing for the safety both of our companion and our camp. We were still nearly two thousand feet above it and could not possibly reach it for two hours.

As we drew near we heard a whistle coming seemingly out of the middle of the smoke and wondered what it might mean. Did it mean that Somerville was surrounded by the fire and that the whistle was his farewell?—first a long blast, then a pause, then several long blasts and silence.

As we came nearer we whistled and shouted, but could get no answer. Smoke still hung round, and we could not see the place where we had pitched camp. I threw down under a conspicuous tree the vast bundle of specimens with which I was encumbered, and gingerly we picked our way among the ashes. The fire had passed rapidly over a large area of ground, leaving a black ash and little smouldering tussocks of rush. Many of the senecios and lobelias still looked green in the heart and I hoped that they would quickly recover.

It was only with difficulty that we found the site of our camp, locating it by means of a prominent rock nearby. There we found the remains of our tent all flat

upon the ground: canvas, beds, bedding, clothes, everything had been completely burned! 'Where is Paul?'
exclaimed Buxton. There were no signs of our companion. Fearfully, fearfully we poked among the ashes,
a small pile of debris hardly now raised above the level
of the ground. As we poked, little charred masses of
blankets and beds burst into flame and then died down
again. What had that whistle betokened? Still, surely he
must have escaped down the valley, perhaps even to the
lake camp. We found nothing gruesome, only a few
metal fittings, a twisted thermometer and a half-burnt,
half-roasted slab of Cadbury's nut-milk chocolate. The
roasted part we ate gingerly; it tasted extremely good,
almost a second discovery of roast pork.

In a little pile in front of the tent was Paul Somerville's
box, with drawing paper, curiously unharmed, possible
since there had been a clear space around it. Here also
was a slightly burned box of pots and pans, and a little
apart a pot with some duck in it, which we had intended
to have for supper. Now it was covered with a film of
black soot.

Still anxious about our companion, we hurried down
to the lower camp by the seventh lake; our anxiety over-
came our natural weariness and kept us going at a steady
pace. Still, we felt in our hearts that whatever had
happened, this must be the end of the expedition. Just
before dark, and about a mile from the camp, a search
party of boys and porters met us and told us that he
had returned safely to the lower camp and was unharmed.
The whistle he had sounded had meant that he was
clearing out. They all condoled with us on our loss very
charmingly and later offered us back many of the extra
clothes that we had given them for the expedition when
they saw that so many of ours had been burnt.

Half an hour later we staggered into camp and heard
the tale of the great fire, sitting over another large fire,

which had been made to keep us warm in place of the burnt blankets. Here also we got our cup of tea, the making of which had caused the fire. Apparently, a kindly thought had prompted our friend to light a small fire in order to boil water for tea. A clear space had been made as usual. But he had not reckoned for the wind, which came down on him in a sudden gust, sweeping the flame almost horizontally along the ground until it caught the neighbouring tussocks of rush. At first the wind had blown the fire away from the camp, and he had hoped the tent would escape. Then suddenly the wind had changed, and the fire, now considerable in extent, had swept down on the camp. Frenzied cutting of the tussocks and beating around the tent had proved of no avail, and he was forced to retire, leaving the tent in flames. The cartridges were going off, popping and banging every moment, as the fire reached them. By now he was almost surrounded by the fire. Truly a Mephistophelean spectacle! He blew his whistle, thinking thereby to let us know that he was clearing out. Then he had to run to escape the flames. In such a situation man is completely helpless, a terrible and humiliating thought, and an experience which he will never forget. At intervals our glances would stray anxiously to the tussocks at the edge, fearful that history might be repeated. The space had, however, been well cleared and there was no danger.

There is a tradition that high mountains jealously defend their summits. Ruwenzori had smiled on us and made our ascent easy; by her very smile she had dried up the vegetation to such an unusual extent that the fire had spread very rapidly and allowed her to hit back at us in a way quite unexpected. Most fortunately, all our specimens and most of the exposed photographic plates had been left at the lower camp, and so we had lost nothing irreplaceable. I rescued a precious notebook from the ashes, all black at the edges, but still legible for the most part. It still smells of burning, a horrid souvenir.

Only one tent had been burnt, so that we still had a second in which we were able to pass the nights, huddling together like three sardines for warmth, and using a spare outer tent-fly as a common blanket. Still, many Ruwenzori travellers have fared far worse, and we were thankful that we were enabled to carry on in this way. Much to the surprise of our porters, who hoped for an immediate descent, we resolved to make a second attempt on the peak.

We again moved up to the site by the fourth lake and pitched a camp just out of reach of the burnt area, though it was impossible to get out of sight of it as we would have liked. Although it had covered a large area the fire had swept quickly over it. Already the centres of the lobelias were beginning to show their green again, and I did not think it would be long before all traces of a burnt landscape were gone. From there we made an ascent of Weismann peak the following morning, being only the second party to do so. We followed the former route up to a point west of the third lake right to the foot of the glacier. Here we found two pools, presumably the first two lakes recorded by Dr. Humphreys. Probably their size varies somewhat with the melting of the snow. Into the first lake ran a trickle emerging from under the snout of the glacier, and this was evidently the source of the Nyamgasani river. The glacier had obviously retreated recently, and there was a large expanse of ice and rock visible, quite smooth and sloping at a very steep angle. The glacier was of an unusual shape, having diminished so much that it was now broader than it was long.

Having no rope or ice axes, we did not venture on to the glacier, but found a way to the peak round the west, crossing some easy rocks and a small snowfield. The way presented no mountaineering difficulties. On the top we found a small cairn built by Dr. Humphreys with a note to say that it was the Weismann peak and that he had made an ascent with George Oliver. We were thankful that we had struck the right place at last. There was a most magnificent view. All the snow peaks were visible and between them great gorges. Between Mt. Stanley and Mt. Baker we saw the two small lakes recorded by the Duke of the Abruzzi, and away to the west another lake. Margherita, the highest point of the range, was clear; its great glaciers sparkled in the sun with that intensity which is only really found in the tropics. As we looked, a great black-and-white crow sailed over our heads and floated away towards Mt. Baker. The air was gloriously crisp, although icy cold, and we all felt more sparkling than we had done for some days. Somerville even frisked about like a young lamb, at just over 15,000 feet, too.

He had taken a challenge from Capt. Chapman that he would bathe and roll in the snow. The witness was to be a photograph. He was keen to carry out the challenge, but I had only three unused plates left, and refused to use one on his exhibition. Our spare clothes, also, were all burnt; so the bathe was passed over, rather a relief, since the temperature was well below freezing and the wind icy cold. My three unexposed plates I arranged with great care, sad that they were three and not three dozen. There were many things which must needs then remain as a memory only: the vast expanses of mountain to the west and south of us; the Namwamba valley, where our companions had been, and the attractive little ice 'penitentes' which had formed round each blade of grass at the foot of the glacier.

Somerville declared that the peaks did not compose well and refused to draw a line—such is an artist's privilege. Like the view from many high peaks, it was overpowering when we saw it. Looking at the photographs afterwards I am rather inclined to agree with Somerville.

One more day only was spent at the lake camp, and then we moved down the mountain as quickly as possible. The porters were keen to get home and willingly concurred; in fact, even sometimes suggested the possibility of double marches. We could not help thinking of the analogy of the horse returning to its stable. So much had been burnt and so much eaten that our loads were fewer and lighter. By now our wardrobes were very comic. Buxton, in particular, had a pair of ragged woollen pyjamas, half-burnt and hanging in long streamers, which he wore instead of an overcoat. He had pulled them out of the wreckage after the fire. I wished that a plate had been left me to record those superb pyjamas. Sleepless nights also emphasized the reliance which we had placed in our sleeping bags, which were far warmer and pleasanter than a multitude of blankets. At night we put on every available garment we could to try to keep warm; one had several old shirts, another an old overcoat, another grey flannels and half-burnt pyjamas. It was a case of dressing up for bed instead of the more usual taking off of clothes.

Considerable brightness among the porters was occasioned by the arrival of a load of meat. An almost incredible amount was eaten in one evening. Five days later, descending over six thousand feet, we reached Chapman's high camp at last, and found him delighted at our successful trip and relieved at our safe return. Somerville accompanied the porters. He reported that they came into camp, swinging along at a good pace, all shouting and singing, happy at their return. Next day came the sad business of paying them all off and saying goodbye. I sat at a long table, computing days against each man, while Somerville doled out to each a pile of shillings, quite considerable in some cases. Unfortunately for them, the local chief had seized his opportunity and was present, raking in the money for poll taxes as soon as we had paid it out. Still, they all got something after allowing for his depredations. It was, indeed, a lucky windfall for the chief, and must have saved him many weary miles of trudging about the mountains after his money.

That day I paid my last visit to the forest, and was rewarded by finding *Thunbergianthus*, the plant for which I had perilously carried my head in the air for much of the expedition. It is a very rampant and woody climber with gigantic pink flowers. Incidentally, the form found by us in the Nyamgasani has flowers twice as large as the previously recorded form. I was led to it by a few fallen blooms on the ground. After a search of the apparent greenness above, we managed to pull the right rope and brought down a whole mass. In the tropics this is often the method by which flowers of trees and lianas are found. But from below, the flowers in the upper layers of the forest are often almost invisible, and it is extremely difficult to decide to which tree they belong. We experienced the same difficulty in the rain forests of Borneo, where it frequently took us a quarter of an hour to decide which tree to cut down. *Thunbergianthus* is only recorded from Ruwenzori in East Africa. The mountain has a number of such endemic species and even genera. The only other known species of *Thunbergianthus* is recorded from the island of St. Thomas, off the west coast of Africa, but it is doubtful whether the two are really sufficiently similar to be put rightly into the same genus.

CHAPTER IV

AFRICA SMOKES

Africa was burning, 'burning bright in the darkness of the night'. When we descended from the mountain the dry weather had begun in the plains. The face of the country had changed. The air was hot and stifling, thick with smoke from the grass fires. Before, we had been able to see Lake George clearly. Now, we could not see a quarter of that distance. Every year a large part of the grassland of Uganda is burnt so as to provide young grass for grazing. It is successful in places, but in places where the vegetation is open, the erosion of the soil is greatly increased, while the fire prevents the further spread of forests by destroying all seedling trees. Since forest tends to increase rainfall and humidity, the burning is not always completely desirable. All over the country this has been the practice for generations, and the administration needs must smile on it. Everything was dry like tinder. As we moved along the track, Chapman put a match to grass by the side of the path in a patch still unburnt. Immediately it went up in flames. Quickly there was a vast conflagration. Everything seemed bare and black, but still the grass would grow again within a few weeks. In spite of the huge fires, the people very seldom lose their huts or their bananas.

Below us they were threshing beans in a field. Somerville was very much impressed by the rhythmical motion of the beaters. A hole had been made. The women gathered the beans and placed them above the hole. On each side stood a man with a long stick. Then they threshed the beans, swinging their sticks as two men with sledge-hammers or axes. It was a primitive but effective method. At the end there was a clear pile of beans where the hole had been.

That evening Somerville drew my attention to a small cloud, gleaming golden in the gap between the hills to the west, as the low sun shone on it. It was a curious cloud, more a golden haze than a thick cloud. It seemed to be moving slowly towards us down the valley. 'What is it, Patrick?' Somerville asked curiously. I could not say. A hand telescope revealed that the cloud was composed of a multitude of small particles, which I soon guessed to be locusts. Buxton confirmed this. Soon a few outlying ones arrived. For those who may not be familiar with the actual beast, I may say that the locust is a gigantic and vigorously flying grasshopper. Next morning we woke up to find ourselves enveloped in a swarm of them. All the morning it came and went. Sometimes the insects seemed to be flying round in circles, but the general trend was down the valley. The sky was darkened and the air seemed literally black with them, a premature twilight. Whenever we moved outside they would beat against our faces and bodies, smack in their aimless flight. It was a most extraordinary spectacle, the abundance of Nature in her most devastating mood. The ground was covered with the locusts. They rose like a wave in front of us. The little boys waved sticks in the air, knocking down half a dozen with every stroke. At last the swarm passed, leaving in their wake a thick sprinkling of stragglers. In many parts of Uganda fried locusts are sold in the markets and are considered a delicacy. But still there hovered over us a large flock of kites and storks, picking up locusts, sinister as they swept round the sky in wonderful, smooth, apparently effortless circles. That evening one of the boys brought a stork into the hut. The stork had apparently eaten so many locusts that it had fallen insensible out of a tree. Apart from a somewhat natural disinclination to eat anything further, he was uninjured. We gave the boy fifty cents and took possession of the bird. He was a magnificent fellow, white with pink legs and bill, a migratory species from Europe, we were told. After a few days he became quite tame and recovered the use of his legs. He would allow Somerville to stroke him under the chin and even seemed to enjoy it. When we had taken some photographs we encouraged him to go off again, and this he did.

From Edwards in the Namwamba we now heard news. They had also been successful in reaching the snows, and had climbed Okuleba, the Observation peak. They had looked over into the Nyamgasani valley, hoping to see signs of our tents, but had seen none. By now Taylor had returned to Kampala, but Edwards was still in the district.

After the mountain, Chapman's house was a wonderful place of rest and peace, where I sat long hours placidly changing the papers between which the plant specimens were pressed, and sorting the damp from the dry.

We did not feel inclined to face the rickety bridge again, but drove out along the twenty miles of private road which Chapman had made. I had cunningly left Boanerges at the top of a steep hill, so we had merely to give her a push to the edge and then let her run down to start. Africa had by many bitter lessons taught me the value of a good hill in starting a car. The grass fires were still burning around. I had visions of being held up by a barrage of fire. However, we made our way through without incident, although in several places we had to pass through patches where the grass was still smouldering and bursting into occasional small tongues of flame. Rush tactics, however, carried us through without harm. Sometimes the fire seemed to be all round us, but some fate looked after us and always a way, albeit a smouldering way, was open before us.

The Nyamgasani route cannot be considered the shortest or the best way to the highest peaks of Mt. Baker and Mt. Stanley, but for beauty of scenery it is probably unsurpassed in the whole mountain. At the end of it there is a pleasant climb on to the snows of Weismann peak, from which a superb view of all the highest peaks can be obtained on a clear day. Good rock climbing there would be in plenty among the peaks at the head of the valley, and the majority of these are still unclimbed, many even unnamed.

Weather on Ruwenzori has recently been raised from a conclusion of 'perpetually bad' to one of more uncertainty. Our experience of six weeks of fine sunny weather would suggest that midwinter, end of December to beginning of February, is the best time to visit the mountain. Probably, also, the southern end, the Nyamgasani end, has more dry weather than the centre or the North, since it abuts on the very dry country around Katwe and Lake Edward. Chapman reported that the rain began again a week after we left, and had not stopped by June; so our experience can only be described as providential. He reported also that it rained all the following winter. After midwinter, it is probable that midsummer is the best season.

The advisability of having some responsible person, preferably a European, in charge of a base camp cannot be over emphasized for any expedition wanting to stay more than a couple of weeks in the higher zones. Of course, without path-cutting the ascent would be very much quicker, but the vegetation grows so quickly over old paths that fresh cutting is nearly always necessary. His presence would inspire the porters with confidence that their next load of food would come up safely. Also, in his absence, porters sent down with stuff and instructed to return with food would be liable to spend several days making merry at their homes before returning, if, indeed, they ever did return. Our debt to Captain Chapman is very great in this respect.

As long as the Bakonjo are pampered a bit, they will probably behave well; but it is necessary to remember that porterage on Ruwenzori is not such an easy matter as porterage on Elgon or one of the other mountains. The Bakonjo are a more primitive people than most of the tribes of Uganda; they have a certain natural fear of the spirits of the mountain. Indeed, the atmosphere of the mountain is very strong. This can only be countered by their belief and implicit trust in their employer and their certainty that they will not be left without food or shelter in the colder parts. We were most fortunate in having no serious injury or illness among any of the porters or among ourselves. The tent-fly which we carried as a shelter for them was much appreciated. It was better than the rock shelters, and made us independent of them. I would unhesitatingly recommend other expeditions to take the same. It is not necessary to take poles for it. Bamboos, giant heather or groundsel poles can always be cut. An ice-axe for climbing might be desirable on the glaciers, but for the forest a bamboo stick is by far the most suitable weapon, a good long one which can be poked deep into the treacherous carpet of moss in front to discover firm footholds and empty drops.

Ruwenzori seems the only mountain which we visited which has a definite personality; it was the only mountain which really had something to say to the traveller: sometimes the word was incredibly hostile, like a terrifying ogre to a small child; sometimes it was a friendly welcome, dignified and courteous, as some beautiful but elderly lady welcoming her grandchildren. Although the silence was intense, we never felt that the mountain was passive. It was awake and watched our every movement. The high moss forest on Mt. Dulit, in Borneo, had this same personality, but I have never felt it on the other mountains of Africa, or in the lowland forests of Borneo or in the Alps. It is a feeling partly induced by bizarreness of vegetation, by snaky and luxuriant growth combined with mist, damp and cold; but it is also a feeling of personality, aliveness, resident in the mountain, something part of it and not entirely dependent on a superficial covering of vegetation. It is a feeling not only of mystery and weirdness, but also of allurement and stimulation, which spurs on the traveller and will always summon him back again. I believe the Arctic often exerts this same weird fascination on her devotees. Ruwenzori is the only one of the mountains we visited to which I am really anxious to return. There is still much to be done there.

CHAPTER V

SAFARI ON MOUNT ELGON

VERY different from the rugged Ruwenzori was Elgon, the mountain on the borders of Eastern Uganda and Kenya, which formed the scene of our first, and also my last, mountain safari in East Africa. Elgon, called by the local people 'Masawa', has one of the largest craters in the world. The volcano has long been extinct, and the crater is now occupied by a large marsh over five miles in diameter. From a distance the mountain looks like a great somnambulant whale, with a long flat back. On the crater rim are the highest peaks, several of which are over 14,000 feet above sea-level. Around the crater is a great expanse of high moorland. In many parts it is really very similar in appearance to the moors of Dartmoor or the highlands of Scotland. Only the gigantic heathers, the bizarre and grotesque groundsels, and the pretentious spiky obelisks of the giant lobelias remind us that we are not in England, but high on a mountain of tropical Africa within one degree of the Equator.

August 1934 had just begun when we left Serere, the Government experimental farm in Bugishu. We all looked forward eagerly to our first safari in Africa. We were a party of five: Ford, Somerville, and myself, Hansford, the Government mycologist, who most nobly undertook and efficiently carried out the organization of the porters and camps, and Hancock, who had visited the mountain before and wanted to introduce us to some of the more striking plants.

It was nearly eighty miles from Serere to Budadiri, the first camp, where the road ended, but we covered the distance in only two hours in Hansford's fast car. The first part of the road was flat and dead straight, and the country seemed very bare. It undoubtedly had suffered from deforestation and soil erosion to no small degree, and Hancock whispered in my ear that this was not entirely unconnected with the well-meaning, but in this case rather misguided, attempts of the British administration to introduce English methods of cultivation. English agriculture rests largely on the plough, and so the first natural inclination is to suggest that African agriculture must do the same. While ploughing opens up large areas, it necessitates cutting down all trees, and in some cases, especially where the soil is light, there is not enough natural regeneration of vegetation to prevent erosion, the soil being washed away by the torrential rains, which quickly score channels through open ground. When the soil is bare, also, the invaluable top layer of humus is quickly broken down by the hot sun. The traditional methods of the tilling of the soil by Africans, in Buganda province particularly, resemble more our idea of cottage horticulture than agriculture. At no time is a large area of ground bare of crops. The crops are so mixed and interplanted that there is always something on the land. After sixty miles of this road we turned off along a side road and began gradually to climb. The way led through masses of *Spathodea* trees, very gay with their vast scarlet flowers, and then through groves of bananas, wet with rain, emerald green and silver where the sun shone on them, and made glistening bright their high lights. Uganda is kind to her travellers. The roads are excellent, and on many of them it is possible to maintain quite as high an average speed as on English roads. It is only in wet weather that it is necessary to go really slowly for fear of skidding.

The Chief of Budadiri was waiting for us. In most parts of Uganda there is a regular hierarchy of chiefs, from the muruka chief, who controls only one village and is under the gombolola chief. He is in charge of a group of villages, and is, in his turn, under the saza chief, who is in control of a large district, maybe as large as an English county, and is a most important person.

This chief was tall and dignified. With a kindly smile he told us that the porters had been warned, and that all would be ready for us to set off early the next morning. As we drove into the camp a drum somewhere began to beat, doubtless telling the district of our arrival. The 'ngoma' drum, popularly called a 'tom-tom' in England, is still the messenger boy of much of Africa. It is a round, squat-shaped drum, and is deeper in tone than the tall 'ngalabi', or dancing drum.

Budadiri was a fine starting point. Elgon seemed to hang right over it, dark with storm clouds, below which the bananas, lit by the low sun, gleamed with a metallic intensity. The rest-houses are very numerous in this district. They consist generally of a square building of hard mud and wattles with a thatched roof and a verandah. An excellent floor is made of dried cow-dung, sometimes with a thin covering of sand on top. The majority are unfurnished, and the visitor brings his own bed and staff. They are maintained by the local chiefs for the benefit of visiting Government officers, but are also available for other visitors when not required for officials.

On Elgon a number of these rest-houses have been built as pleasure camps for officials on holiday and for visitors. They are an asset to the local people, since they bring many visitors, which means employment as porters and a sale for some of their surplus foodstuffs, such as chickens, eggs, milk, sheep and cows. To the camp is generally attached a small vegetable garden which the camp-keeper tends. Budadiri, as also Butandiga, our next camp, both had fine strawberry beds.

Beside the camp there flowed a turbulent river, fresh from the mountain. The air was crisp and cold, and brightened us after the anæmic languor of Serere.

Somerville pranced joyfully about the camp, brandishing a paint brush, until Hancock laughingly exclaimed: 'Who will rid me of this turbulent artist?' Outside in the roadway danced a man with a feather in his cap, bells on his legs and a dagger in his hand. He pranced up and down while Ford endeavoured to take a photograph. Hancock said that he was probably a Kavirondo boy from Kenya.

Hansford believed in an early start, doubtless quite rightly, but he was not really popular when he woke us all up before dawn and ruthlessly turned us out in the cold, packing up the camp into loads of forty and fifty pounds each. I was surprised at the apparent weight and bulk of some of these, but he said they were all right, and so it proved. Still, we were grateful to him when we arrived at our next camp by ten o'clock in the morning, having accomplished the stretch in the cool; besides, a midday storm occurred nearly every day that we were on the mountain, and it was well to make camp before then, if possible.

The loads were all lined up, with the porters standing, each man opposite a load, a long row of dusky silhouettes in the dawning light. Always on Elgon more porters turned up than we had asked the chief for, or were able to employ. Each man is paid from thirty to fifty cents according to the length of the journey. Each day's march up the mountain ascends about two thousand feet and takes two and a half to three hours. The path is good.

We always had one load which was conspicuously smaller than the others, and always the same comedy would be enacted over it. Before the porters lined up by the loads we would see one man eyeing it with interest. Then he would move along the line until he came opposite it. Sometimes several would try to get it. Wreathed with smiles, the successful man would try his load. Then gradually the smile would die as he realized that the load was far from being a light one, as he had anticipated. It was the cash box and contained the cents to pay the porters. They are paid at the end of each day and in cents, some in ten-cent pieces, and some in strings of one-cent pieces. Imagine the weight of ten pounds worth of pennies, and then you will have some idea of the weight of the cash box at the start. Its weight, of course, diminished day by day. The victim never got any sympathy from his fellows, who thoroughly enjoyed the joke and chaffed him over it. It was a perennial comedy. Few things seemed to appeal more to their sense of humour than the sight of the discomfited man who had schemed for an extra light load and got a heavy one. The same man never carried it twice!

First the porters filed out and then we followed, after counting the number. There were fifty-two. At the gate were waiting the local chief and the camp attendant to say good-bye. They were clothed in the white kansu of ceremony, the garb usually worn by chiefs. It may cover a multitude of rags underneath. So prevalent is it that one early traveller described the country as 'White cotton nightgown country'. The description was somewhat apt. The kansu doesn't resemble anything else so closely.

The way led directly over a bridge made of wattles and having the appearance of matting. Still, it only sagged slightly as we crossed. Thence we wandered through the banana groves. The banana is probably the most abundant tree in Uganda, tree by courtesy only because it does not make a woody trunk. It forms the chief article of diet of many of the tribes, who use the green bananas and boil them into a mass called matoke. This is almost tasteless, and has the appearance and consistency of boiled parsnips. The Baganda peoples like it better than any other food and will always be unhappy if they cannot get it. The quantity consumed is enormous. As far as I could gather, one man eats a 'hand', that is the very large bunch as it grows on the tree, in about three days. In Baganda there is a great variety of sauces used to flavour the matoke, and a good wife is one who can make a large number. Some have called the Baganda an unnaturally apathetic race, and have attributed it to this banana eating. I doubt, though, whether there is any real ground for this supposition. Also, the majority of the work in the fields is done in the early morning before the European is abroad. The Africans mostly will work when they want food. They have the extra incentive of money to buy luxuries such as tea and sugar, bicycles or clothes. Now that there are more luxuries to buy and taxes to pay, it is probable that more work is done.

In Uganda the bananas have many other uses besides that of food. Drink in the form of a mildly intoxicating and highly popular banana beer is made from them. From the stems fibre is torn to serve as string and rope. Many of our loads were tied up with it. From the leaf little bags and baskets are made. Even milk is brought in a neat little bag made from a banana leaf, which has a pleasing freshness and cleanness. A single banana leaf also makes an excellent umbrella. One man enumerated the varied uses to which the banana is put in Uganda. There were over forty.

The banana groves are a wonderful sight in the early morning as the sun gleams through the great leaves with a translucent shimmer of green. The stems are pillars marked with deep crimson and rich purple near the base, on which the flecks of sunlight play, joyful in the beauty of the morning.

There are many people about, and as we pass the men smile, while the women often kneel, murmuring a shy greeting, 'Merembe, Bwana, Merembe'. Some of the women carry heavy loads of bananas. The majority of these must have been much heavier than any of our loads, and they carried them further than any of our porters went in a day. Many of these loads must have been over a hundred pounds in weight, yet they sturdily marched uphill with them, and rested less often than our porters or ourselves. In addition, they often carried a baby on their backs. No wonder the women age prematurely.

Coffee-growing is a recently established industry among the Bagishu of this district, which is too high for cotton. We passed several patches and were surprised at the health and vigour of the plants. Many coffee-growers in East Africa have attempted to ward off 'native' competition by scares that the African would not be able to manage the crop, that it would become diseased and would then spread disease to the European farms. Such healthy plantations show that these scares are without any foundation, at any rate as regards the people of this district. There is a scheme for co-operative preparation of the berries and selling, and a European adviser, who is actually employed and paid by the 'native' administration. This new industry is undoubtedly a great asset to the district.

Although South America now produces the largest part of the world's supply of coffee, the plant is really a native of tropical Africa, being found wild in the forests of Uganda and the Congo, and in Abyssinia. Undoubtedly its use is very ancient among the Abyssinians and the Arabs. In flower, the coffee is very beautiful. The whole bush is covered with a mass of white starlike flowers whose scent is overpowering.

The wanderings of economic plants are full of interest. The fruiting banana, which forms the main diet of many of the Uganda tribes, is not a native of Africa, but has been imported. The wild, native banana of Africa, the species we found in Ruwenzori, bears no fleshy fruit, and it is fairly certain that the cultivated type has not been derived from it.

63

The path up this part of the mountain was a wide grass track. From a distance it looked like a vertical ribbon of green, so steep was the mountain here. We zigzagged slowly up, until we emerged at Butandiga Camp. This is placed on a ridge looking out over the valley from which we had come, and to the mountains of Nkokonjeru on the other side. We had passed the upper limit of the bananas, and below us they seemed as an emerald-green sea in which the round huts nestled like little islands.

After lunch we were disturbed by a sound of jangling bells and of shrill whistling. We emerged from the camp and found three young men attired with plumes on their heads and bells on their legs, rolling and prancing down the hill towards us. Their attitude looked fierce and threatening, but this was only pretence, part of the game. They were preparing for the circumcision cere-mony. In their mouths were whistles which they blew as they danced, or rather pranced, about the mountain. The movement was very ungainly and primitive, merely a heavy kind of prancing and musical staggering about, which carried them from village to village. For several months before the ceremony they did no work, but pranced about in this way, working up an ecstasy. We met another party six weeks later at Sipi, further round the mountain. They were in even finer attire and had worked themselves up almost into a state of ecstatic furore for the ceremony. We heard that for the actual operation many now fled into European hospitals rather than face the elders of their tribe, some of whom still operated with primitive sharp stones and pieces of blunt, rusty steel. The young men learn hygiene in their schools, and many are even now being trained to act as medical dressers and even doctors. So naturally they are not content any longer to undergo the unnecessarily unhygienic and painful operation as performed by the elders. Still probably the elders would say that pain was an important moral part of the ceremony. We all turned out to photograph them.

In England many know the common orange balsam which grows by the side of the streams. We had heard of the big white balsam of the African mountains, but had not seen it before. In the afternoon Hansford went out for a short walk and came back with a bunch of it, the flowers of which far exceeded my expectations. They were very large and shaped like a white butterfly. The centre was streaked with crimson markings, and behind the flower was a spur several inches in length. The whole was borne on a long, thin stem, well clear of the foliage, so that it seemed to float in the air. The plant grows to a height of six to eight feet, and I feel should be a great success in English gardens if it could be acclimatised there. Underground, it has great tubers like a dahlia, and it is possible that it might be grown under similar conditions. It is rightly called *Impatiens elegantissima*. Very few plants get such a definite superlative from the botanist who names them. I am excluding the fancy names and descriptions of horticulturists, who have often lost their effect through using over-lavish superlatives. Film-makers and publishers have in the same way done much to kill the golden goose of the exact meaning of words.

From Butandiga we set out again at dawn for the next camp. This time Hancock and I decided to collect plants and insects on the way up, and did not attempt to keep pace with the porters. I have always found botany and photography excellent excuses for not hurrying on a mountain. Hancock also has a lame leg, a relic of an old hunting accident, and found it difficult to get along as fast as any of the porters, although he allowed it to interfere wonderfully little with his climbing.

At Butandiga I had annexed 'Bunny'. His real name was Bunyara, and he was a Bugishu, short, stocky, and with a pleasant smile. His job was to shadow me, carrying plant-presses, cameras, coats, and other light impedimenta, act as scale-object for my plant photographs, and generally prevent me from getting lost. He proved a great treasure and stayed with me all this trip. Most of the characteristic plants of the mountain are so large that a human figure makes the best scale-object, and it is an advantage to have the same figure always for purposes of comparison.

We visited the giant balsam and collected seed in a little tin. All the balsams have explosive seed mechanisms. As soon as one lays hands on a nice fat capsule, it explodes and scatters the seeds far and wide. The only course is to pick most gingerly those capsules which are approaching ripeness and incarcerate them in a small tin, where they may explode without loss of the seed. After explosion the seed may be safely dried in the sun. The very generic name 'Impatiens' refers to the hasty character of these seed vessels.

Our path lay along the edge of a cliff face, and every few moments some new plant caught our eye and made us stray first to right and then to left. First there was a fine Hypericum tree, the St. John's Wort, with big yellow flowers overhanging the cliff. In England we have no Hypericum larger than a small shrub in cultivation. This plant was a fair sized tree with flowers as large as the common 'Rose of Sharon'. Then a gleam of orange at the edge of the forest attracted us. It was *Canarina Eminii*, an epiphytic plant, growing in the fork of a tree. It had long, pendulous branches, attractive glaucous leaves, and large bell-shaped flowers, orange striped with crimson. They hung from the tree in festoons like bells and tinsel on a Christmas tree. The discovery of a fine plant like this gives a real thrill to the botanist, just as a fine head marks a red-letter day for the hunter, or a fine picture for the art collector.

66

Much of the forest had been cut for wood, and the ground is now covered with a low scrub of bracken and everlasting flowers. The ubiquity of the bracken is astonishing; exactly as in England, it has colonized those mountains wherever a space has been cleared. A few patches of forest remained, and there we found a Crinum lily, *Crinum Johnstonii*, with bulbs the size of a man's head and enormous shiny leaves like a monstrous four-foot of emerald strap. The flowers were large and good, white with a purple streak down the centre of each petal. For their vast bulbs alone they would always be a curiosity.

Nestling in a gulley we also found tree ferns, a type of plant to which I have always been much attached. This was a species with enormous fronds, but with a villainously prickly trunk which effectively discouraged any close attachment in the literal sense. From below the fronds spread out like great green stars and presented a magnificent model for the type of photograph known as 'Art in Nature', although probably better described as 'Nature in Art'.

Bulambuli camp proved to be a square bungalow in the middle of a grass clearing fenced with stockade. Behind it began the bamboo forest. Our collecting activities had delayed us, and already the equipment had been largely unpacked, the porters paid off, and the subsidiary tent for scientific work and meals was being erected in the compound.

In front, Hansford was bargaining for some meat. It was live meat, and stood, a short row of cattle, before the camp. At last a moderate-sized beast was procured for a modest sum. I think it was twenty-five shillings. We ate beef for the rest of the time we were on the mountain: beef liver for breakfast, beef and suet pudding for every other meal. It was cold, and this was Hansford's choice. He said there was nothing better for keeping warm than a good stodgy suet pudding, and plenty of it.

He carried these principles so much into practice that one day he and the other senior member of the expedition were unable to move outside the camp. Light-hearted friends whispered that it was over-eating. They themselves faintly suggested the altitude.

From grossness it is well to proceed to lightness. The graceful, feathery plumes of the bamboos are the very acme of lightness. As the sunlight flicks with brightness the golden canes, the wind makes the green leaflets to dance, and the stems to bend. Yet for all its apparent frailty a bamboo never breaks. The Chinese are the only race who have really appreciated the beauty of the bamboo. Many of their painters have devoted their whole lives to the rendering of the subtle patterns of the bamboo, and their countrymen have not considered their lives wasted. As Laurence Binyon writes in one of his beautiful essays on Chinese Art, 'The bamboo symbolises for the Chinese the noble character bending before adversity but never broken'.

Yet the Chinese seem never to have penetrated right into the bamboo forest, but always to have hovered on the edge, preferring the individual to the mass. Inside it is dark, damp, mysterious and gloomy; little sunlight penetrates.

All the afternoon it rained, but in the evening the sky cleared and we wandered out along the path, hoping to see the first giant groundsels (Senecio). The reality, however, surpassed our expectation. There he stood at a twist of the path, where it descended into a dip to cross a small stream by a rickety bridge; a veritable tree over twenty feet high, branched, gaunt, and with a certain pathetic, bizarre and indescribable look of unreality as of an old man, transported from another planet or age and set down to confront the present world. 'Senex', indeed, means an old man, and these trees are veritable 'Old men of the Mountains'.

The trunks are twisted and contorted often into all manner of weird shapes, so that some become almost more animal than vegetable; they are surmounted by mops of foliage, like great lax cabbages. The leaves are very large, sometimes three feet in length, and of a rather fierce shade of metallic green. The old leaves do not fall, but remain attached to the tree, dangling as a dead, slowly-decaying mass around the trunk below the rosette. Sometimes they are so numerous that the whole trunk becomes a pillar of dead leaves with a central core.

At Bulambuli there were none in flower, but higher up in the alpine moorland zone we found the giant groundsels flowering frantically. From the centre of the cabbage crown would emerge a vast spike, sometimes three or four feet high and branched repeatedly. The flowers of the higher species were very similar to those of the common English groundsel, except for size and number, but those of the lower species were always much more ornamental, having long ray florets (petals to the non-botanist) like the ragwort or yellow garden daisy. Some of these flowers would be an inch and a half in diameter, and one spike would bear a hundred or more, so that the effect was very striking.

At first the sight of the giant groundsels dominated us, and their bizarreness seemed an ever-exciting and thrilling wonder, but after a few days we began to accept them as part of the landscape, to expect their presence rather than their absence. Even so soon does habit dull over the sense of wonder. On each mountain they were slightly different in appearance and each time thrilled us anew when we came upon them after an interval in the plains. There are no canaries on the African mountains, the more the pity. These giant groundsels would feed all the canaries in the world for a time approaching all eternity, but I suspect that they would be pretty tough and would give our poor canaries a bad tummy ache. Rabbits might cope with the leaves, but would be unable to touch them growing, owing to the trunk. Still, there are no rabbits on the African mountains, although there are a few hares. In fact, there are very few large animals. An occasional duiker, a small kind of antelope, may be seen bounding away, and also there is the hyrax, and that is probably about all on this side of Elgon. On the other side some big game has been recorded from the forests, and on some of the other mountains there are elephants, buffalo and gorilla. Leopards may be seen occasionally.

In the dead leaves of the giant groundsels, and in the crown-like rosettes, the entomologists found a paradise of peculiar insects. They suggested that some of the beetles were confined to these plants and were closely related to species and genera found in Europe but absent from the rest of Africa. When really roused, an entomologist can be far more destructive than a botanist. The botanist takes a few leaves and flowers off a tree, or maybe takes a whole herb, but at any rate he leaves few signs of his depredations. The entomologist may dismember the whole plant, tearing it ferociously from limb to limb into little pieces and then, worst of all, he leaves the pieces scattered about. Still, one hopes that in Africa these remains may quickly rot and disappear, although they will not do so as quickly on the mountains as in the warmer lowlands.

At first the sight of the giant groundsel dominated us and we looked nowhere else for a few minutes. When we did look around, we saw a large open patch in the bamboo forest through which flowed a small stream. It was so floriferous as to suggest a garden. It was a glorious place. There were· rosettes of giant lobelia and glistening leaves and incipient flower spikes, great monsters six feet high and far removed from the little blue plant which we all associate in England with the name Lobelia. Still, there were some little lobelias of the more constitutional type also. There were also red-hot-pokers with attractive loose and graceful spikes of flower, brilliant shell-pink terrestrial orchids, large white begonias and little violets extraordinarily like the English violet, but, alas, without the supreme gift of scent. Then, in the background, a giant Rubus formed the kitchen garden. If we except the fact that the flower was yellow and the fruit a brilliant scarlet, we might have called it a blackberry. The berry was large and the flavour strong, although rather sour. The very young bamboo shoots also make an excellent vegetable dish. They should be peeled of their outer sheath and then treated like asparagus, for which they would indeed make an excellent African substitute. There is just a suggestion of the peculiar asparagus flavour mingled with a rather strong nutty flavour, which makes them attractive. They must, though, be served only when they are very young. When older they become very hard. We missed the blue gentians and rhododendrons of the Alps and the Himalayas. There are none in East Africa.

As evening drew on, the coolness of night at nine thousand feet came down on us, and we were glad to close up the tent and sit around the special primus which Hancock had bought after his first mountain trip. On top of the primus was suspended a metal ball, which quickly became red hot. Behind that was a reflector. This stove was also a great advantage for drying the plants, and in particular the leaves of the giant groundsels. At the base, these are covered with a curious gelatinous mass, some of which we were able to scrape off. The rest we dried by toasting before the primus stove. It must have been a comic sight. There were Hancock and I sitting one on either side of the stove, each holding out the base of a big leaf in front of the fire. This work required careful judgement, since they had to be toasted just sufficiently to dry off the gelatinous slime, but not so much as to shrivel the leaves.

Plant collecting suggests a pleasant, lazy occupation. In fact it is just the opposite. In new areas it is necessary to cover as much ground as possible so as to gather a representative collection of all the plants over all the different zones and associations. In a general collection such as ours, all the plants had to be gathered, not only those with showy flowers, as many collectors delight to do. Often the duller specimens turn out to be the least known and most interesting when they reach the herbarium. After gathering, each plant must be put either between paper or into a tin box, so as to keep it from wilting. It is impossible to make a satisfactory specimen from a plant which has begun to wilt or shrivel up. Several specimens of each plant are required, so that they may be distributed among different herbaria. In camp each piece must be carefully laid out between paper so as to make a well-shaped specimen. All this makes a very considerable difference to the man who eventually names the specimens. It is very difficult sometimes to identify with any certainty specimens where there is only a fragment of the plant, or where it is very shrivelled. On each specimen a label must be tied with a number, and this number must correspond with the number under which the field notes are written in the book. These should be as full as possible. Details as to place collected, altitude, date, size of plant, colour of flower and whether it is very common or rare are all desirable. Some collectors do not even mention whether their specimens come from a tree or a small herb a few inches high. Though often it is apparent from the specimens, it is not always so.

Such work would occupy my every evening. On this particular occasion I was lucky in having a skilled African assistant, 'Musoke', who had worked for a forestry officer, then on leave. He was able to lay out the plants as specimens, taking great trouble to arrange them nicely. Then he would bring them to me for the addition of numbers and notes, and after that he would watch over their drying, tenderly, like an old nurse over her children. Often this drying took several days, and, in a few extreme cases, weeks in this damp atmosphere, and, if possible, each day until they are dry the paper of the specimens should be changed. The papers can be dried by the fire and used again. Fire heat can also be used on the specimens, but not too vigorously. Such is the plant collector's life. The actual collecting of seeds for growing in England is the least, although perhaps the most fascinating, part of it. The number of attractive horti-cultural plants growing in England is so vast that I feel we should not try to increase it greatly without adding something really good. The seeds finally sent are generally only those which have given me a real thrill and about the merits of which I am certain. If I am doubtful about its merit, even to a slight degree, I find it is nearly always better to discard it. A few plants and bulbs, of course, are collected blind for trial in England, but only a very few, and those with some ground for enthusiasm. Not only plants with large flowers are valuable. Plants with decorative foliage or bizarre habit are equally of interest.

'Musoke', my Muganda assistant, was a real treasure, always careful, always smiling, and always ready to help. The name 'Musoke' means 'The Rainbow'. He was also an excellent cook and was useful as personal boy. He had to some extent the habit of anticipating one's needs. When I came in cold and wet, he would arrive within a minute with a cup of steaming hot coffee or cocoa and a dry set of clothes. Then he would bring fresh paper for the plants and begin on them immediately while I changed. He was also one of the few Africans I met who seemed to appreciate the beauty of scenery. Before the waterfall at Sipi he would stand, rapt in admiration and quite silent. We were very sorry to lose him when his master returned from leave in October, for such boys are rare among the Africans, or, for that matter, among the Europeans.

At another table Hancock and Ford pinned and sorted insects. In a corner bubbled the Berlese funnel, an ingenious toy for the extraction of insects from plant material, such as the dead senecio leaves and the lobelia spikes. The material was placed on a sieve at the top of the funnel, which consisted of two layers of copper between which was a space into which boiling water was poured. The heat from the warm copper made the insects emerge from their hiding places in the spikes and fall downwards through the funnel into a jar of alcohol, which was ready below. So complete specimens were obtained with little trouble. Hansford called it 'The bloody lazy' funnel in jest, for its name, 'Berlese', saying that it did the entomologist's work for him. It was also excellent for warming the hands. Every time we packed up to move, it seemed fated to be left to the last, and then we would go along the line looking for a light load on to which it could be tied like a great burnished clown's cap. It was not a bit heavy, but somewhat bulky, and consequently unpopular with the porters.

From Bulambuli our next move brought us to Mudange, a thatched grass 'banda' hut at 11,000 feet, with rather more draught than grass.

On the ascent we found some positively immense plants of the giant *Lobelia gibberoa* deep in the bamboo forest. We measured several. They were twenty-five feet in height and had a flower spike of just over six feet. Unfortunately the flower spike is of a rather dingy greenish-yellow colour, but the whole contour of the plant is magnificent, like a vegetable soldier with an upraised lance. It is not really a tree or even a shrub, but an overgrown herb.

Just before 10,000 feet the bamboo changed into a forest of giant heathers and tree groundsels. Then abruptly this forest ended and we emerged into the open moorland zone which covers all the top of the mountain. It was exactly Exmoor or the Highlands of Scotland; only in places the illusion was broken by the giant groundsels, lobelias and heathers. Patches of pale pink everlastings with grey foliage stood up against a black sky under which the sun gleamed with a parting and fugitive intensity. These everlastings did not have the extreme abomination of stiffness which we associate with the Victorian drawing room during the winter months. Their pink and grey made a very pleasant harmony.

From the camp at Mudange we could see right up to Jackson's summit, a great, cold Catherine-wheel of a rock. It is not actually the highest point of the mountain, but it is the point usually ascended, since it is only a few hours' distance from Mudange, and presents no climbing difficulties. Its height is 13,600 feet, while the highest summit, a rock further round to the south-east on the crater rim, is 14,100 feet. The African name for this highest point is 'Wagagai', and this name has now been adopted by the Uganda Survey Department. We did not, however, hear any African name used either for Jackson's summit or for the highest point. In the opposite direction we could look down the mountain and see Lake Salisbury, shining in the evening light as a streak of silver against the horizon.

In the afternoon I set out for a short stroll up the mountain, this time not taking Bunny with me. It was a fine interval, but I did not expect to get far. Suddenly I came round a corner on to a most extraordinary sight. In the middle of a small round marsh beside the path were raised a number of green obelisk-like pillars, as in a cemetery. They were five or six feet high and dotted about irregularly. The spikes were round and about a foot in diameter. On closer acquaintance these proved to be yet another species of giant lobelia, *Lobelia elgonensis*. The actual flowers were deep blue, and they could just be seen peeping out among the stiff green bracts, which gave the obelisk its green appearance. The spikes were stiff and rigid, as if they had been made of marble and then coloured green.

I was much excited with this discovery and gathered a whole plant under my arm, like a great baby, and with it marched proudly back to camp. It proved a heavy burden, but luckily the distance to the camp was only about a quarter of a mile. It is, of course, impossible to press such a monster whole, so he was cut into thin longitudinal slices; indeed a sad ending for such a noble monument; but still in his sliced and pressed form he should last for centuries, while in' his other he would only last for a year or two.

From Mudange we made an expedition to Jackson's summit, on the top of which we found a cairn and a cigarette tin simply full of names of those who had ascended before. The actual Jackson's summit is composed of granite rocks and there is no difficulty in clambering up. Here the tree groundsels were clothed all in white. A thick, short, silvery-white, furry indumentum covered their leaves and younger stems. On other mountains we found some even more thickly covered, as if they had put on a thick shaggy fur coat over the leaves. It was particularly thick on the under surfaces. We found the same ascending series of giant groundsels on each mountain, lowest the plant with thin leaves, lanky stems and loose rosettes and long ray florets, then in the main alpine zone a species with thicker leaves, more compact rosettes, some indumentum (hairiness) on the leaves and short ray florets. Then, highest of all, the species with thick leathery leaves, thick felt-like or woolly indumentum and compact rosettes and no ray florets. There was yet another species of giant lobelia, *Lobelia Telekii*, the last on this mountain. It has long hairy bracts, drooping and covering the blue flowers, which give it the appearance of a gigantic woolly caterpillar, petrified and stood on end.

Below the summit is a small tarn, a mysterious, a lonely, a solitary, and indeed a most ghostly place, as the mists play around and unroll to leave the melancholy and twisted groundsels and the funereal lobelias standing in silhouette, a dark fringe against a white background. The tarn is very shallow, grass-bottomed for the most part, and in it were reflected the weird plants twisted even more weirdly if that were possible. Around, the sun and the mist played games with each other, until one could verily feel the ghosts on the move. What a perfect setting for a ghost story this tarn would make! The teller could easily make it black and bottomless. I have seldom seen a place more desolate and more haunting. Only Ruwenzori could surpass it, and probably the higher zones of Ruwenzori would be voted the most mysterious and unearthly places in the whole of Africa by those few who have visited them.

The next day I went to the crater, parting half-way from Ford and Somerville, who wished to visit the tarn and Jackson's summit again; Ford to fish for water beetles and other aquatic beasts in the waters of the mysterious tarn, Somerville to sketch some of the patterns and colours of the lichens on the rocks below Jackson's summit. These were truly glorious and spread over the rocks like patterned Persian carpets.

I had fondly imagined the crater to be only a little way, but it was a good four hours' trek before Bunny and I topped the last grass slope and ran down into the hollow. It was a great flat marshy expanse, dotted with giant groundsels and lobelias and encircled with low hills which formed the rim. Here I found the largest groundsel I had seen on the mountain, a veritable ancient of years and rightly placed in this, which is probably the largest crater in the world. The size and majesty suggested the idea, 'What king lies buried here?'

It was fiendishly cold, and soon a biting hailstorm came on. Bunny cowered under a rock, using his grey blanket as a hood and remaining motionless, until he almost became part of the landscape, while I made a hasty search for plants. There is now no permanent snow on Elgon, but these hailstorms are not infrequent, and sometimes the white crystals lie on the ground for some hours. It freezes practically every night. In the past there has certainly been an icecap and permanent snow on the mountain, and traces can be found of old moraines. This is true of all the African equatorial mountains. Formerly the icecaps extended several thousand feet lower than to-day, and those without any permanent snow had an appreciable white glaciation. Still those days were long ago, but probably not so long ago as the earliest traces of man which have been found in Africa. With pluvial and interpluvial periods, the icecaps alternately retreated and advanced. This is an age of retreat.

After a few minutes of chilly waiting, Bunny was glad to don a spare coat of mine, and we beat a hasty retreat, without finding any further vegetable wonders. In spite of the long trek, somewhat unexpectedly I found myself back in camp before Ford and Somerville, but they returned a few minutes later, very cold and wet, but having spent a very happy morning.

During my absence one of the porters had brought in a pair of the most fascinating little chameleons, all scaly and nobbly, like miniature dragons. Their most usual colour was an emerald shade of green, but their changes of colour were clearly marked as we put them on different backgrounds. On the mixed background they behaved with equanimity and did not pine away through trying to become several colours at once, as some writers, more sensational than truthful, have asserted. According to the Africans, these chameleons are common on the mountain, and they frequently brought them in to us, but I do not think that one of us ever found one for himself. The eyesight of the African for anything that moves is phenomenal. They are, however, afraid of the chameleons, and will never actually touch the animals, always carrying them gingerly on the end of a long branch. They say that the chameleon can give them leprosy. The chameleon sits perfectly still, melting into his surroundings, until a fly comes close, when, like lightning, out shoots a tongue almost as long as the beast, and scoops in the fly, and the chameleon rolls round his eyes with joy. These eyes are most fascinating, projecting right out and pivoting presumably on the ball-and-socket principle so that they can look in all directions. The two eyes do not necessarily always look in the same direction. In fact, they generally squint most fiendishly.

The high moorland of Elgon is not unvisited by the Africans as are the similar zones on the other high equatorial mountains we visited. The Wanderobo people graze their cattle over it, and a path has long existed through the crater between Kenya and Uganda. The mountain does not seem to be in any way a place of fear or veneration as are Ruwenzori and Mount Kenya. On the Kenya side of Elgon trout have been introduced into several of the rivers, and there is good fishing, popular among the European settlers, who are numerous on the Kenya side.

Late in the afternoon we were summoned from the tent by cries, and found that one of the boys' huts was blazing merrily. There was no one, and presumably nothing left inside, and we all stood around watching the fire, the porters dancing round and thoroughly enjoying it. There was nothing else to be done, and certainly it made a fine blaze. As there were several other huts into which they could crowd the matter was in no way serious. Unanimously and loudly they blamed Jaimsie, the skinner, a boy who had come to Hancock after experience with an American expedition. He was, alas, universally unpopular, for he had derived the worst effects from his contacts with civilization. He would try to lord it over the other boys, which they naturally resented. Now they seized their opportunity, and all swore that the fire had been caused by Jaimsie and by Jaimsie alone, that he had put the rat skins too near the fire, which all Africans build inside every hut. How the nearness of the rats had caused the general conflagration no one explained. Probably the fire had been much too large and they all had sat round enjoying it. At any rate, next day Jaimsie was sent off with two porters to gather grass and stakes and rebuild the hut, which was finished in a few hours.

We only stayed four days at Mudange, the highest camp, and from there easily made a double march downhill to Butandiga. We had hoped to cross the top of the mountain and return down one of the other slopes, but the weather was so bad that the porters would not agree to attempt it.

Our mountain trip ended in a drive in torrents of rain from Budadiri back to Serere. Boanerges had returned and seemed now to go; but in a storm water leaked in everywhere, in at the sides and through the division in the windscreen, until I was almost temporarily blinded and we had to creep slowly along. Besides, the

Indian lorry with the camp equipment had broken down, and Boanerges was now loaded up with bedding and specimens to the maximum. After dark the Uganda roads seem to drag on indefinitely. In the eastern province they are excruciatingly long and featureless, but generally dead straight. However, we arrived by ten o'clock, more than two hours after Hansford with his eight-cylinder Ford.

Elgon had, indeed, been a pleasant introduction to the equatorial mountains. It must be recorded as a very easy and comfortable mountain to climb, hardly deserving the name of expedition, for it was rather a holiday excursion. I paid two more visits to the mountain, one with Somerville, in September, to the magnificent waterfall at Sipi, and the second alone, the following May, to Mudange for botanical work, hoping to find out how much some of my marked plants of Senecio and Lobelia had grown in the interval. I found that the lower ones had grown considerably, all the marked leaves, which had been green and fresh in August, being dead by the following May.

CHAPTER VI

TOBOGGANING TOTOS

In September, Somerville and I set out for Sipi with Kabanga, a cheerful boy from the Entomological Department, lent us for the express purpose of catching as many mountain rats as possible and collecting the parasites off them for a flea census which is being made. Rat fleas carry plague, and it is most desirable to obtain as much knowledge as possible about them and the rats, their hosts.

Ford had intended to come with us, but, most unfortunately, at the last moment had to retire into hospital with a bad attack of fever, combined with a heavy infection of hookworm, which may have been a relic from our former expedition to Borneo. We were very sad at having to leave him behind, but knew that he would be in good hands at Namirembe, the big C.M.S. hospital, which is established with much success in the lee of the cathedral on one of the seven hills of Kampala.

Musoke, as cook and plant boy, preceded us in a bus with the rest of the camp equipment, such as a safari table, camp chairs, his cooking utensils, and, most important of all, several 'debies'. These are empty four-gallon petrol or paraffin tins, and are universally used throughout East Africa for carrying water and for cooking. In them he would bake excellent bread and cook quite a variety of dishes. These buses now permeate the country; the majority are owned and managed by Indians, and sweep about nearly always full to overflowing with both Africans and Indians and all manner of odd baggage. Some are old and decrepit, and driven to the danger of the public, but the majority are fairly new and powerful, and reasonably driven. Fares are moderate, and often Europeans are to be seen travelling by them, sitting in front beside the driver.

Somerville stayed on a few days at Mbale to paint a general view of the mountain from the plains, a great long whale-back of a mountain, too large and too long to be very impressive. So, unfortunately, he did not witness the comic episode of the bottle of Macnab's Sparkling Beer. Tired after a long day of driving to and from Mbale, I felt pleased when the boy brought me at supper time a bottle conspicuously labelled 'Macnab's Sparkling Beer'. I could not remember having ordered any beer, which is terribly expensive in the tropics, about half a crown for a pint bottle; but, somewhat absentmindedly, I poured a little out into the tumbler. This was not a glass one, but of the so-called unbreakable type, made, I believe, out of dried milk. It was strongly coloured and opaque, so that I could not clearly see what I had poured into the bottom, only noting that it failed to produce any froth, and thinking that Mr. Macnab's sparkling beer must have lost its sparkle and be a bit flat.

Then I took a gulp, and it was one of the nastiest things I have ever done. The taste was even worse than that of the fieriest and freshest of the Borneo rice spirit. It was methylated spirit, not the pure, colourless spirit used for scientific purposes, but the mauve commercial stuff, seemingly extra-adulterated against African use. Quickly I spat it out and rinsed my mouth many times with water, but it was some time before it really seemed clean again. Now I remembered ordering some spirit for lighting the lamps. No one had bothered to change the label, hence the sorry disappointment at the bottle of Macnab's Sparkling Beer. Why my sense of smell did not warn me in time I have never been able to think.

All round the north and west sides of the mountain, between six and seven thousand feet, is a rampart of cliffs. Sipi camp was situated almost on the top of this; and from its verandah a grass lawn slopes down to the cliff edge, which is protected by a very frail looking fence. Here the cliff curves into a kind of horseshoe shaped amphitheatre; in the centre of the horseshoe is the Sipi waterfall, one of the finest and best known bits of Uganda. The volume of water is not great, but it falls sheer, and without break, for several hundred feet, a white ribbon disappearing into a cloud of spray in a rocky basin, hidden by the luxuriant forest. Behind the waterfall the cliff is a strong reddish orange, and down it black streaks extend, probably the result of an increase in the volume of water during wet weather. On this vivid background the sun plays through the water and casts an ever-changing and ever-fascinating pattern of light and shadow. We found that it was very restful and peaceful to sit and watch it pouring over, night and day, into the dark forest below. A waterfall is, perhaps, the most dominating of all Nature's spectacles, the only one in the face of which it is absolutely impossible to say anything at all. At night, when the moon shone on this silvery water, it almost suggested at times a willowy and stately figure surveying the mysterious forest below. Round the amphitheatre, and then down the side of the cliff, there is a small track which brings one suddenly out through the forest to the stupendous spectacle of the fall from below. Against the clouds of spray stand out the vast translucent leaves of the wild banana, in colour a brilliant, almost emerald green, yet possessing something of the quality of jade. The leaf is edged with pink border and centred with pink midrib. This species has no stem, but the leaves emerge from a great deep crimson cradle of the old leaf bases. Against the wild bananas the darker green and more definite form of the Dracaenas add a richness and a more rigid geometrical design to the scene. Here the waterfall is far too dominating a spectacle to permit of any consecutive thought. The noise, coupled with the sight, seems to shatter the brain into submission to its power. Where the ribbon of water touched the rocks at the base it broke into a cloud of spray. Into this shower I ventured, and my unwitting, though thorough, showerbath was rewarded with a fine pink balsam, which seemed to grow only in the spray.

Soon Somerville, with his usual magnetism, attracted round him a crowd of little Totos, children from the neighbouring village. They would stand enthralled while he painted, and be delighted if they were given a brush to play with or a spare piece of board to carry. One of them, nervous, but oh, so proud, was chosen as a model and sat for his portrait. He had a fine face, not so thick and heavy as the very negroid stock, but longer, thinner, and with a fair mixture of that more cultured asceticism which the Hamitic stock brought down from the north and mingled lavishly with the Bantu blood.

When Somerville went out several of these charming Totos would always follow him, and little hands would help by pushing him behind as he toiled uphill. For me they would sometimes bring back flowers, particularly a fine blue Coleus which grew up to eight feet and was used for fences round the village.

When we read and lunched, the Totos would amuse themselves by tobogganing on the steep grass slope in front of the camp, rolling off just before they came to the fence. Sometimes they would have races, and quite a row of steeds would be lined up. I was always left in fear that one of them would barge hard into the fence and go through over the cliff. However, such a calamity never occurred. I daresay that in reality the bushes with which that part of the cliff was covered would quickly have 'fielded' him. The toboggans represented yet another use for the ubiquitous banana. They were made from the great curved bases of the leaves, cut from

85

the part where they begin to encircle each other to form the so-called trunk. They were most effective. The majority were single-seaters, but a few two-seaters were seen in action as well. Smooth and slippery, they speed down the hillside a roaring, laughing, shouting mass until, near the edge, all the little feet suddenly shoot down as brakes and the little dark bodies roll off into a revolving ball of tangled limbs and laughter.

We were visited again by a party of the 'Circumcision' dancers, even finer in their plumes than before. Their time was now near. Somerville persuaded one, a superb figure of a young man, to sit for his portrait; but he would sit so stiffly and unnaturally, rigid as if carved from a marble block, that a natural drawing was difficult. Even such an exemplary habit as sitting still while your portrait is being painted can be carried to excess. He was of a very typical negroid stock, with broad face, wide, flat nose and massive lips. His black hair was raised erect in front, and round it were two bands which formed the base of a magnificent headdress of white nodding plumes. Round his neck was a collar of brilliant green cloth; against his rich chocolate skin he wore a series of chains of red, blue, and white beads, encircling his chest. On his shoulders were epaulettes of blue serge, while at his elbows were fringes of white plumes. In his hand he carried a baton ending in a very fine black plume, which he whisked about, even as particular ladies whisk the dust from precious furniture and china. On his thighs were bells which jangled whenever he moved, and on one of the bead chains was suspended a whistle, which was more often to be found between his lips than elsewhere.

Others were even more bizarre and grotesque in their attire. One had a kilt of dried leaves and a black mask. Another a pair of motor goggles, and the Old Boy's tie of a prominent English public school. I won't mention which, I do not suppose he had been there. The whole village assembled by the camp to give them welcome, in their midst a fine banner made out of an old white blanket with a coloured border. The women, clothed in lengths of fine printed cottons, added a touch of colour to the scene.

Sipi was quite a large village, and the grain huts nearby made a second village. Many of the slopes above the falls were covered with bananas. Beneath them the ground was carpeted with the most beautiful little balsam flowers shading from a delicate mauvish white to a deep pink. In their many and varied colours Somerville said he could feel a link with the murmurings of the streams which were ever with us. So wide was the expanse of bananas that it would have been easy to lose oneself among them. Once I thought my guide did so, but after much wandering we emerged safely, and he would never admit to having missed the way, even slightly. Above the bananas was yet another waterfall.

The grain huts were built in rows like a little village. They looked like huts turned upside down, being round at the base, but with a large projecting roof on top. The edges of this roof were supported by all manner of odd stakes, which gave to it a crazy picturesqueness. They were all thatched and yellow from the dried grass and fibre with which they were built. They were supported off the ground by piles so that the rats should not invade them and eat the precious grain. Harvesting of the millet grain was going on while we were there, but I do not know whether they got enough to fill all the grain huts or how many were full already. It would, indeed, have been a rich village with all those huts full of grain and so large an expanse of bananas.

On this expedition to the mountain we saw no Europeans; but another time, when I was on the mountain alone, I met a white Father, an elderly, bearded figure in a white cassock and with a staff in his hand, striding about, followed by his flock as some shepherd of old. He was a most kindly and charming man, and had lived the greater part of his life in Africa.

The people, as usual, were attractive and friendly, and many visited us, being, perhaps, less shy of two Bwanas alone than of a whole camp full of white men. One day an old man came to us leading a sheep, brown, as are most African sheep. I never saw a white one in Uganda. The man had a really fine profile, like that which I would assign by imagination to some old Hebrew prophet as he stood with his staff and his sheep on a short string. The sheep was for sale. and he asked some quite modest price for it; I rather think it was six shillings. But, alas, we did not want a sheep that day. There were plenty of eggs and milk, and still the memory of Hansford's beef diet lingered from our first trip to the mountain.

I enjoyed the time at Sipi more than any portion so far of the expedition. It was so quiet and peaceful. No eternal small 'shauries' disturbed me, as on most of the bigger safaris. Every one around us seemed happy and contented.

But, after a fortnight, the time came to depart, and we ran down the two thousand feet to pick up Boanerges in the camp garage at the bottom. But that fickle power was in one of her most recalcitrant moods. The brute was pushed nearly half a mile downhill, but nothing would induce her engine to start. Her battery had run down during our absence, and in no way could we induce sufficient electricity to start the car. Finally we had to send off a boy on a bicycle to Mbale for another car and a battery. Luckily, it is quite a common sight in East Africa to see a car being pushed in an endeavour to start. We were not exceptional in that way. On these occasions we had to try to be patient and remember that, after all, she had only cost thirty pounds and had since then been driven some thousand miles. After some hours the mechanic arrived and started Boanerges with leads from the battery on his car, and we followed him slowly back to the town.

By making use of the ferry over a projecting arm of Lake Kioga we were saved a long detour. It also gave an hour's rest from driving and was intrinsically fascinating. Although the distance must be easily less than a mile, the passage takes an hour. The ferry consists of a raft, buoyed on a pair of canoes, and the car is run on with great care over a board. Very heavy vehicles, such as laden lorries, have frequently caused trouble by sinking the ferries, the raft quietly subsiding into the water beneath them. But we were well below that weight.

The ferry is poled across by four men in much the same way as a wherry is quanted on the Norfolk Broads. They stride the length of the ferry, then shove in the poles and push, walking the opposite way. At each turn they slap their feet down on the boards with resounding whacks, and then about-turn to repeat the process. Doubtless, from always going barefooted, their soles are so hard that it does not hurt them. To music in the form of shouts and resounding and reiterated songs they keep time with their feet and enliven the passage. The African always feels, and rightly, I think, that a hard job of work goes easier with the aid of rhythmical music to which his movements can conform.

The passage was beautiful; we passed slowly along a narrow channel of water cut between two eight-foot banks of papyrus swamp. Blue water lilies fringed the swamp, which was fascinating in the mystery of its dark depths and tangled luxuriance. We heard rustling in the depths and felt that it might herald the emergence of any manner of vast or weird beast, even a survival from the great swamps of prehistoric times. However, nothing followed the rustle but a flock of little birds.

In addition to my three visits to the mountain, Edwards and Taylor paid a visit of several weeks to the eastern slopes, on the Kenya side, after they had returned from Ruwenzori in February of the following year. They were accompanied and guided by Mr. T. H. E. Jackson, of Kitale.

The Kenya slopes are even more gradual than the Uganda ones. There is much more open grassland, much less forest and bamboo. There are a number of European farms on the lower slopes, and the land is reputed to be some of the best in Kenya, growing good coffee and many other crops, also European plants such as roses with great luxuriance.

They climbed two peaks on the eastern rim of the crater, but did not actually descend into it, since they found such a multitude of interesting things to keep them on the slopes. One of the peaks they climbed had a flat top, and the natives called it aptly 'Mesa', which means 'the table'. The other was thought at the time to be Jackson's summit; but Jackson's summit is really in Uganda, and this was another peak; it was possibly a few metres higher than the actual Jackson's summit.

Many interesting flies were obtained, including some associated specially with the tree senecios and giant lobelias. Some of these were surprisingly similar to British species. They also found some unusual wingless flies of a strange 'spiderlike' type in a high patch of forest.

Mount Elgon is famous for its vast caves, and several of these on the eastern side were visited. At the back of one cave, in complete darkness, was a large pool in which white frogs were swimming. These are probably an albino form of the common Xenopus frog. Bats, too, were present in great numbers. Edwards is reputed to have caught about a hundred in one swoop of his butterfly net. Then the party settled down to disentangle and delouse the squeaking mass. Bat parasites always seem popular among systematic zoologists and entomologists. Many are most peculiar.

It is from some of the former cave dwellers on the southern slopes, the El Gonyi, that the mountain takes its name. The more general native name is Masawa, and the people living near the mountain never use the name Elgon. It is a pity that the wrong one of the two names was selected for our maps.

CHAPTER VII

LOST IN THE BAMBOOS

A LAND full of little round volcanic hills and very blue, winding lakes, a landscape dominated by three great volcanoes, a land where eggs can be bought a hundred for a shilling, milk two cents—about a farthing —a quart, and a live sheep for half a crown to five shillings, a land where the skin is given back to act as clothing for the African vendor.

Such was our objective, the Birunga or Mfumbiro Mountains, old volcanoes which cross the floor of the Western Rift Valley in the south-west corner of Uganda. We decided to confine our attention to the three which can actually be climbed from Uganda territory. These are Muhavura, 13,547 feet, Mgahinga, 11,400 feet, and Sabinio, 11,960 feet. The boundary between Uganda and Belgian Ruanda passes through their summits. Mfumbiro means 'The Cooker' in Luganda, and probably referred to their former volcanic activity. Captain J. E. T. Phillips, in the *Geographical Journal*, suggests the name 'The cooking place of God'.

Somerville, most unfortunately, was not able to come, a fact which I have ever since regretted, for the country was some of the most picturesque in Uganda. Edwards and Taylor left in one car with E. G. Gibbins, an assistant in the laboratory of the Medical Department at Mulago. He had been given leave to accompany us for this trip and for part of the time on Ruwenzori. Ford and I did not take Boanerges, but had a fine staff car which was lent temporarily to the expedition. The African driver was both fast and good, so that it was a relief to be able to look at the scenery for once instead of wondering always whether Boanerges would get

up the next hill or not. All the boys and the equipment followed in a lorry, again a noble loan from the
Uganda Government; so we were well equipped with
transport.

Lake Nabugabo was our first stopping place. It is a
delightful little lake cut off from Lake Victoria by a wide
strip of marsh. It would be an ideal place for large-scale
biological experiments on fish for Lake Victoria, as I
believe Dr. Worthington suggested. It has also the
especial merit of being free from crocodiles, and having
a sandy bottom. A delightful rest-house has been built
right down by the water's edge, where miniature waves
break on a little sandy beach.

From Nabugabo we went on to Kabale, the adminis-
trative centre of the Kigesi district. There we had to wait
a day for the arrival of the lorry. The country was very
beautiful. There were innumerable green hills, like the
green hills of Ireland, and valleys, often filled with
papyrus swamps. We visited one such valley at Butale,
where the papyrus swamp had the unusual addition of
giant lobelias, a curious mixture of the lowland with
the mountain vegetation, which we saw nowhere else.
Mr. Rogers, the District Officer, and Mr. Wykeham, the
Agricultural Officer, received us most kindly and helped
us. There was a comfortable, though small, hotel, where
we had our meals, and a rest-house next door where we
slept. The hotel was then full for the duck shooting,
which had just been opened on Lake Bunyoni.

Mr. Rogers accompanied us the first part of the way
to Mabungo Camp along the magnificent new road
which has been built connecting Uganda with Ruchuru
and thence Lake Kivu and the Belgian Congo. It is a
wonderful engineering feat, for the country is very
mountainous. It is probably the most beautiful district
in Uganda. The scenery is fine, the soil is rich, the food
cheap, and the climate mild.

Soon we caught a glimpse of the three mountains, the volcanic triplets. Muhavura is an almost perfect cone, rising very steeply 7,000 feet from the plain; Mgahinga, a dumpy mountain by its side—rather like a blancmange in shape; but Sabinio is a rugged mountain with a chain of five rocky peaks, particularly exciting, since we had been told at Kabale that it had only been climbed two or, at the most, three times before. Unlike the more recent, and therefore more perfect, cones of Muhavura and Mgahinga, it is an ancient volcano and much dissected with many precipitous gorges.

None of these three volcanoes have erupted within memory time, but the native name 'Muhavura' means 'The Beacon', and old men of the district told us that they remembered seeing a glow from the top when they were children. One old man also said that his father had told him of a similar glow from Mgahinga. Away in the Congo on dark nights we were able to see a slight glow in the sky, the reflection from the crater of Mount Nyamlagira.

Mabungo camp was built on the side of one of the little volcanic hills which are so characteristic of the district. Their sides had been cultivated in patches, which gave them the appearance of being closely draped with a patchwork quilt. Any bare patches of brown or red earth stood out vividly. The system of supports and terracing is very slight, and it surprised me that their plots did not often slip down the steep sides of the hills, but we saw no signs of this happening. The lava plain which stretched between us and the mountains was thickly cultivated. Young crops of peas, beans, potatoes and maize, as well as other good things, were growing vigorously. This country has been called 'the Roof of Africa'. Near here are some of the most distant and ultimate sources, both of the Congo and the Nile. Neither of these rivers can be said to have a single source.

The inhabitants of this district are Banyaruanda. Many are distinguished by their peculiar style of hair-dressing. In the centre is left a ridge, while beside it are shaved two wide bands. The centre thus gives somewhat the effect of a cockscomb. Their dress is still chiefly skins of goat and sheep. In Uganda both are brown, and I found it difficult to tell them apart at a distance.

The next morning we all set out for Muhavura, the foot of which was an hour's march away. Edwards and Taylor decided to take the small tent and spend a night on the flank of the mountain, while Ford and I planned to return to Mabungo, getting to the top meanwhile if we could. A small train of porters carried tents and bedding.

We ascended from the north-east, following a ridge, and gradually worked round a bit to the east side. On all this flank the mountain is so steep that there are no bamboos, only short grass and, in places, a low scrub dominated by shrubby St. John's Wort. It had been reported that there was no flat spot on the mountain where a tent could well be pitched, and, indeed, it looked so from below. However, after about four hours we reached a tolerably level site on a small shoulder of the mountain and were able to make enough room to pitch a tent after smoothing the ground and cutting down some of the higher grass tussocks. We had now reached nearly 11,000 feet. There was no water on the mountain side, and porters had to be sent up to the crater lake at the summit to fetch a supply for the camp. This journey they readily undertook for an additional fifty cents each.

The others stayed round the camp, and with two men I pushed on towards the peak, of which we caught brief glimpses as the clouds moved across. After another hour the giant groundsels began to appear in the gulleys, and above us we could see through the mist stiff pillars, gaunt and mysterious against the skyline, the old flower spikes of *Lobelia Wollastonii*, the finest of all the giant lobelias.

We passed through thickets of the giant groundsels, many of them rising to twenty feet and branching copiously. All the trunks were covered with mosses in thick cushions, and often strangely contorted as in some fairy forest on the pantomime. The bizarre effect was heightened by the straightness of the stiff lobelia spikes, mostly brown and dead. But a few were still flowering, a delicate pale powder-blue and silver where the sun caught the moisture left by the mist. Many must have been twenty feet or more in height. They towered over my head.

Already the effects of the quick climb were beginning to tell, and I had to rest every few minutes. A giant lobelia a hundred yards in front always formed a goal for me, and I would decoy my tired body with 'just so far and no farther'. Then I would rest a moment or two and repeat the process. As we ascended the stages got shorter and shorter. It was not an ideal or correct method of climbing, but it was literally the only one that I could manage at the time.

By now the groundsels had become much smaller. Finally, as we emerged at the top of the cone they were flowering from rosettes scarcely raised above the ground. The leaves below were white with a thick shaggy woolly covering, a characteristic of the species from the highest altitudes. It was very cold and windy, and their leaves were clothed as with a thick fur coat, really not so very unlike the fur of a rabbit.

On the top we found a little crater, almost a perfect circle and holding a small lake about ten yards across, clear and beautifully cold to drink. From below it was quite invisible, and there seemed something odd and unexpected in finding a lake where there looked only a peak.

The clouds hid the greater part of the view from the crater rim, but I had a brief glimpse of a fairylike thicket of senecios and lobelias on the Congo side, which seemed equally steep. Far away on the Uganda side could be seen Lake Bunyoni and Lake Mutanda, appearing as sudden glints of dark blue as the clouds moved and carried gaps above them. A sharp hailstorm caught us on the way down.

In the morning Taylor climbed to the summit after collecting in the groundsel thickets. Edwards told us later that they had been able to see Lake Edward, away to the north. They had spent an extremely cold and sleepless night at their high camp. 'It was paradise', exclaimed one of them after the following night at Mabungo. Ford and I climbed again to the summit a few days later to collect more plants. This time it did not seem such an effort. I suppose we were becoming acclimatised slightly.

Next we turned to Mgahinga, and a camp called Lugezi of bamboo huts was built in a space cleared in the bamboo forest which filled the col between Sabinio and Mgahinga. About seventy men were employed, and in three days' time they had cleared a site and built us seven bamboo huts, the total labour cost being under three pounds. The cook's hut always appeared on fire, since the smoke had to find its way out through the roof. As we walked across the plain, the men returning from tilling their fields would clap their hands in greeting as we passed. It was a charming custom.

Edwards, Taylor and Gibbins went up first to occupy this new camp, and from there climbed Mgahinga, cutting a path through the bamboos, which here form a very dense forest. They reported that it had taken them a long day, and suggested that it might be easier from our side. They had found a pleasant little crater with a marshy lake at the bottom of it, and lots of flowering groundsels and lobelias. They had not reached their camp till after dark, and had been guided back for some of the way only by glowworms held in the hand.

The same day Ford and I went down to Lake Mutanda. The short turf was full of terrestrial orchids, red, orange, and white. Some were very attractive. At the edge of the lake was a papyrus swamp, in which I wallowed for a time after a large yellow orchid. Still, it was a good reward and made fine specimens. A small piece of it is now growing in Surrey.

Ford still wanted to collect insects near Mabungo, so a few days later I set out for Mgahinga without him. He sent his insect boy to collect in the crater, and I took two Banyaruanda, one of whom said that he knew the way and reported that there was a path up from the Mabungo side. But guides in Africa, and, indeed, in most other places, can be divided into two classes: those who don't know the way and tell you so at the beginning, and those who don't know the way and leave you to find it out. Naturally, the latter class is by far the larger. This man belonged to it.

Beside Muhavura, Mgahinga looked a mere pigmy, and the clear atmosphere made it seem ridiculously near.

After nearly two hours' walk across the plain and foothills we entered the bamboos. Quickly the track got less and less, until after a time we realized that there was no track at all. Among the bamboos were most charming glades, bright with everlastings and other flowers. There were numerous tracks of gorillas and elephants, but we never saw any. It was among these mountains that the famous American naturalist, Carl Akeley, studied the gorilla, died and is buried. The great Belgian National Park is only a few miles away across the border. There no shot may be fired. The guide seemed to have a sense of direction like a crooked

98

billiard cue, and we wandered hither and thither, sometimes along an old track, presumably made by an
elephant or a gorilla, more often battling our way through
the bamboos.

The crater was not reached till nearly half-past three.
For the last part of the way I had left the Africans by a
convenient rock and battled my way on alone through
a breast-high thicket of woody undergrowth. The crater
was considerably larger than that of Muhavura, and to
the Congo side the rim fell away, breaking the circle.
On the rim stood up battered tree heathers, twisted and
uneven from the wind and trailing sulphurous streamers
of the yellow lichen known as 'The Old Man's Beard'.
Beside them the lobelias stood erect, stiff, smart and
militant. There was a dark lake at the bottom banked
by a green marsh, pleasant-looking from above, but in
reality very treacherous, as I found after slithering down
the steep sides of the crater.

Time was short and the hour already far later than
I had anticipated; so I made a very hasty collection of
plants and photographs, packed up the kit for the three
men who had joined me at the summit, and hurried
down. For a time we were able to follow the track made
by Edwards and Taylor, but although it led us down, it
led us round the mountain to the wrong side. When
darkness came we were still among the bamboos, and
then we lost the path in a clearing and found it impossible
to follow a track; so we took a course as straight downhill
as we could manage. In the darkness the bamboos looked
grim and menacing. The delicate tracery of the leaflets
was lost and their shoots looked like vast upraised lances,
at a pageant or a review. We saw many taller bamboos,
but I can remember none denser or more monotonous.
In places I had to throw my whole weight against them
before I was able to force a way through. So progress was
slow, but at any rate we did seem to be getting steeply

downhill. Once we fell suddenly down the sheer side of a small ravine and had laboriously to clamber back and seek a way round.

Finally, after some hours of this going, hours which seemed an indefinite age, we emerged on to a grassy plateau, and I thought that the worst time was over. In the day the bamboo forest seemed dim and mysterious enough, but at night it was positively uncanny, and I soon began to find myself imagining faces behind every spike. Alas, the sides of the plateau proved to be so precipitous that we had to work a way round and down again among the bamboos. Up to this time we had been struggling in thick darkness, but now the moon rose, very tardy, and we were able to see enough to find a better way down. Mobungo camp was reached soon after midnight, to my great relief. I was surprised to find that it was not much later.

In the centre of the table was a bottle half-full of whisky, a glass, some water, and round them a row of candles stuck in empty bottles and hurricane lamps. I was glad of it on this occasion. There was nothing else the others could do except put out a light. This they had done and then retired to bed. A throne-like rocking-chair explained that Wykeham, from Kabale, had arrived on a week-end visit to us. We had planned in Kabale to attempt Sabinio together on one of his Sundays, as he expected to be doing a tour in the district. So next day we moved up to Lugezi camp. By now there was quite a big space cleared and a large, but somewhat damp, encampment of tents and bamboo huts.

We learnt there that Edwards, Taylor, and Gibbins had attempted an ascent of Sabinio the previous day and had cut a path through the bamboos. They had reached a large rock at the end of the summit ridge. The actual summit had been continuously covered in mist, and they had not thought fit to venture in such a thick mist along the reputed knife-edged crest of the top. Edwards and Gibbins had spent the night under the rock, but in the morning the mist had shown no signs of clearing and they had come down. They reported a fine sight of the glow from the two live volcanoes, Ninagongo and Nyamlagira.

We were luckier. Before dawn we started from the camp with an electric lantern and torches made from bundles of bamboos. A rather incompetent guide had almost to be pulled out of bed before we could start. We followed the path which had been made by the former party, ascending not straight, but encircling the mountain first through nearly ninety degrees. Among the bamboos the torches flared and flickered mysteriously against the straight stems, and the sparks dropped on the grasses like little twinkling stars. There were numerous tracks of gorilla and elephant and buffalo. Once the second guide exclaimed that elephant was near. We all stopped warily. I got ready the big Reflex camera, but we never saw the elephant. He also pointed out to us the great nests of the gorillas and places where they had recently been feeding on the young bamboo shoots.

He was a funny little fellow, and seemed to know the mountain much better than the real guide. He was nearly a foot shorter than the others and must have been at least half pigmy, if not more. We were now on the borders of the pigmy country. A quaint little face peered out of masses of dark hair. There was something rather animal-like about him. He was dressed in skins and behind him hung down a furry tail. This was actually the tail of the monkey skin out of which his cloak, his bag and his tobacco pouch had been made, but it appeared as if attached to his person. In one hand he carried a smouldering bundle of bamboos, the fire which can be carried for hours; in the other the sickle-shaped 'Panga' chopper with which he cut the stems. These curious

shaped pangas were common. The hook curved round
the bamboo, so that it fell easily, generally with one
stroke, when used with the skill that only the Africans
possess.

Thanks to the path, we reached at 9.45 the rock under
which Edwards had slept and which his party had not
reached until 1.30. Without the path we obviously
could not have done this. It was a large boulder covered
with yellow lichen and slightly sloping, but providing
very meagre protection. Edwards had said that the
lichen had been a delusion, since it had absorbed the
water and then quietly dripped it down their necks.
There was luckily plenty of wood of the tree heathers and
groundsels and they had been able to make a fire. This
we renewed and left the Africans by it, as they did not
evince any desire to come further with us and would
probably have been more nuisance than help without a
rope in a bad place.

The name Sabinio has been derived as meaning 'The
Father of Teeth'. The summits certainly did stick up
from the main ridge and suggested great teeth. We were
now at the end of this ridge. The mist hid from us the
highest point, but it was rolling around fitfully and we
could see a short distance; so we proceeded. The ridge
was not so knife-edged as had been made out, and we
climbed without any very serious difficulty. The one
member of the Alpine Club present, however, would
not allow me to photograph him negotiating the ridge,
saying, without much truth, that his position was not
always consonant with the dignity of that body. A very
faint track was visible along the ridge. It had probably
been made by a mountain leopard, an agile beast.

On either side the mountain fell away in precipitous slopes covered with Senecios and with its
curves formed vast and spectacular arenas. The mist
would reveal to us one arena or one peak at a time as a

curtain rolls back in a theatre, disclosing first one scene, then another. All this made the mountain thrilling, and I think we appreciated it more that way.

On the first summit we waited some time, hoping that the mist would clear, and wondering whether the next peak was higher or not. Finally we decided to go back, but fate, or some imp of fortune, decided otherwise. In the mist our sense of direction had become atrophied; in our intention to go back we went forward, only discovering, after a little distance, that it was not the same way that we had come. Another dark shape appeared in front of us, apparently a peak higher than the one we had climbed; at first it seemed an hallucination, but gradually it assumed reality. This peak we climbed and quickly realized that it must be the real summit. By this time we were thoroughly uncertain of the direction of the rock under which we had left our porters. The mist gave no sign of rising.

Luckily, one member of the party always carried a powerful whistle in his pocket. This he normally used for summoning his boy, and so saved his voice, which was husky owing to a war wound. This he blew vigorously. After a time, faintly came back answering shouts from the porters. They could not have been more than half a mile off in a straight line. So we guided ourselves back, blowing the whistle at intervals and listening for answering shouts. Gradually these got louder and louder. By now I had gathered a large bundle of plants under my arm, and with them I negotiated the rocks delicately and comically. Soon we reached Edwards's rock, under which we lunched.

Wykeham hurried off after lunch to prepare an experiment down below, while we remained for a few more hours in the hope that the mist would clear and we would be able to get some photographs, looking along the whole ridge to the summit.

The descent was rapid, and just after dark we joined Wykeham at Bunagana, the camp on the Congo border, from which it is reputed possible to see all the volcanoes on a clear day. We did not have such a day. Although he had started down several hours before us, he had only arrived about half an hour earlier, since the pigmy guide had lost him among the bamboos. Bunagana is about the same distance from the mountain as the camp we made at Lugezi, and either would make an excellent base. The flora of these mountains was not nearly so rich in numbers of species as that of Elgon or the Aberdares, but their shape precluded the development of an extensive zone of Alpine meadow such as is found on the more easterly ranges. For this very reason their scenic beauty was much greater.

The party broke up a few days later. Ford and I walked back to Kabale by the old track across the hills and by the ferry on Lake Bunyoni. This was the route by which salt from the salt lake at Katwe had long been carried into the Congo. A thriving trade had once existed, but even now it was by no means extinct. Beautiful though the drive along the new road had been, this was an even finer route. It took us three days though, instead of three hours.

Behunge was our first night's destination, a camp set on a high hill. As we arrived the wind whistled around, bending unmercifully the bamboos. Rain had drenched us and we sat shivering, draped in blankets, while our clothes dried. Gradually the wind subsided, the sky lightened and the sun appeared again, but now low, near to the horizon.

Away from us stretched a landscape of little round, almost lunar hills, a landscape bounded only by the three great volcanoes. This aspect of the country reminds us that these volcanoes have been quoted as a rival to Ruwenzori in the probably insoluble problem of

'Where are the Mountains of the Moon?' of Ptolemy and Herodotus.

Descending a thousand feet next morning, we came to the water meadows, spangled with white everlastings and red-hot-pokers, but the season was not right for their full glory. We crossed on an elevated causeway and thence downhill to Bufundi, the beautiful camp set on a promontory jutting right out into Lake Bunyoni. This name means 'The Lake of Little Birds'. Truly in the evening the air is full of a piping and a twittering, but this is caused not by little birds, but by innumerable frogs, which pop up continually among the water lilies which fringe the lake. One of our objects was to make a collection of these frogs for the Museum. Most curiously, in every one we caught there was a white swelling on the eyelids caused by the parasitism of a nematode worm. This feature, as far as I know, is only recorded from Lake Bunyoni. It certainly does not lead to any decrease in the number of frogs, which are as multitudinous as they well could be.

By the light of the moon we caught frogs in a net as they popped up among the large leaves, so plentifully bespangled with little running balls of silver. As we looked back from the camp through an arch of candelabra Euphorbias, the large leaves, so placid and almost motionless on the smooth water, gleamed almost like burnished silver in the moonlight, and seemed to represent the very acme of peace.

Lake Bunyoni has been formed by the damming of a mountain river due to eruptive movements of the earth crust, and is as beautiful as lakes formed in such a way frequently are. It lies surrounded by hills, indented with many deep bays and besprinkled with islands, like Loch Katrine in Scotland. In the evening light the hills and islands even took on the same blue and purple hues of that lake, but in the harder glare of full daylight they are a glorious emerald green. The bays and islands are thickly fringed with blue scented water lilies of a type larger and brighter in colour than any we saw elsewhere. Among them little canoes glide most charmingly. In one end sits a man gently paddling, while the other end, beautifully shaped, glides over the lily leaves. These canoes seemed much more shaped than any others we saw.

In the morning, early, the ferry comes and carries us across, two large canoes paddling alongside each other. Through the islands and water lilies we go. On the largest island has been established a leper hospital, but there is no time to go near it. There are, mercifully, not very many lepers in Uganda.

Lake Bunyoni is certainly the most perfect holiday resort that could be developed for Uganda officials. The green and blue hills and water are a wonderful contrast to the brilliant scarlet tone around Kampala, which stimulates for a time and then jades. There are no crocodiles, and so the bathing is good. Duck shooting has now been opened on the lake during certain seasons. There are no 'sporting' fish at present, but it does not seem unlikely that they can and will be introduced even as the black bass have been introduced into Lake Naivasha. Fifteen hundred feet higher than Kampala the climate is very much cooler.

At Kabale we find the lorry has nearly finished loading up with our goods and petrol, and we clamber aboard. Then a slow and dusty jaunt back to Kampala, through the green hills of Ankole, so like those of Ireland.

CHAPTER VIII

WITH AFRICAN STUDENTS
ON KENYA MOUNTAIN

As a little white lady on a vast platform, a pinnacle on a swollen and tremendous base, stands Kenya mountain. It was not until nearly the end of April that Hancock and I were able to get away for a fortnight there. He had only a short leave from his work as tutor at Makerere College, and so we had to hurry over the trip much more than we would otherwise have done. With us came three boys from his biology class at Makerere, who were keen to learn about mountain vegetation, and Yesero, his African Assistant, who had been trained at Budo School and was inseparable from the three Makerere boys. These three were training to be African schoolmasters, a course in which they are expected to learn a very great deal in a very short time.

After the trip on Mt. Kenya, I planned to pay a short final visit to Mt. Elgon; so I drove as far as Tororo and left the car there, joining the train in which were Hancock and the boys. They had left Kampala an hour and a half before me, but the train in which they were did not arrive till another hour and a half after me at Tororo, although I had not made any particular haste. The country of Uganda is made up of innumerable small hills, and the line seemed to curve round each one of them. It also made a detour almost to Namasagali, the port on Lake Kioga.

Slowly we wandered through the night and through most of the next day down into Kenya, and then up the escarpment to Nairobi. In the last part uphill, the train moved so slowly that often little boys would run alongside asking for cents from the passengers. The European accommodation was quite adequate, but the Africans were very much crushed up together in third-class coaches without any sleeping space, rather too much so, I thought, considering the price of their tickets, which was not small. Still, the railway is a very real blessing to them. In one day it carries them over a stretch that they might have taken a month to walk. Semwanga, the humorist of the party, even murmured to me the quotation from *Julius Cæsar*, 'Let me have men about me that are fat, sleek-headed men and such as sleep o' nights.' He didn't manage to quote it absolutely right, but it was good to see that Shakespeare was sufficiently vivid in their mind for them to refer his words to everyday events and problems. All of these four boys were different from each other. Each had quite as much individuality as an English schoolboy—if not rather more.

From Nairobi we set out by lorry for Nanyuki, where our base was to be. We had only two hours of daylight left, and so slept that night at Thika in the hotel beside the perpetual thunder of the waterfall. It was a very pleasant spot.

The next morning we drove on to Nanyuki, from whence we were expecting to set out up the mountain. Since our time was short and both of us were unfamiliar with the country, we had arranged for a local hotel man to supply the safari equipment and porters, and generally manage the safari for us. Commander Hook was an enthusiast for the mountain; his especial aim was to drive his lorry up as high as possible, and he had already managed to reach 12,000 feet with it on the northern flanks. The great forests of Mt. Kenya are all on the southern and eastern sides, and towards the north the forest belt decreases in breadth and luxuriance until right at the northern end there is no forest, but only short grass all the way up. From this northern flank the country stretches away flat and almost desert-like right up to the Abyssinian border. From the hotel the snow peaks were easily visible, standing out clearly against the sky. The mountain was vast and fine, but it had none of that mysterious grandeur which characterizes Ruwenzori. It is an extinct volcano, and must once have been several thousand feet higher than at present. The snow peaks represent the plug blown up in the vent of the volcano. All the rest of the cone and crater has disappeared. Commander Hook pointed out the main peaks to us, the summit with Batian and Nelion, the two highest peaks which Mackinder named with such a perfect geographical gesture after the two great chiefs and medicine men of the Masai people, Sendeyo, the lesser peak, standing up like a rocky wheel from the flat expanse of moorland. 'There are miles and miles of waste grassland up there,' he said, and we could well believe him. Around Nanyuki there had been a prolonged drought and the grass was very parched and brown.

Many of the Kenya mountain streams have been stocked with trout. The water was very low, but still the pools seemed good and we were able to land a few fish, although they were mostly small. The fish are obviously very numerous, but they are inclined to be rather lean and small. Probably time will remedy their size to some extent. Trout fishing in Kenya is yet very young. Further clearing of the banks where the streams run through the scrub and forest might help their size, since fish food is generally more plentiful in sunny rivers. It would also help the fishermen, but times in Kenya at present are bad, and there is little money to be spent on labour for such things.

Big game is plentiful around Nanyuki. Commander Hook has built a little wooden house high up in a great tree in the forest overlooking a salt lick, where rhino and other animals came frequently for the salt. It is an attractive idea, and we wished that we could have had longer at Nanyuki and spent a night there. He has named it delightfully 'Rhino Look-Out' or 'Honeymoon sky-parlour'.

The next morning we started out in his six-wheeler truck, a heterogeneous load, with boys and porters clinging on to all corners. Those who did not manage to find a place to which to cling had to walk up to the first camp. A pony also followed, which Hancock intended to ride part of the way higher up. Mr. Adrian Van der Westhuizen, Commander Hook's young farm manager, joined the party at Nanyuki. He had never been up the mountain before.

Leaving the road we jogged up the north-western flanks over the short grass until we reached a glade at the beginning of the forest. The height was almost nine thousand feet. Here we made our first camp and Commander Hook left us, promising to return in eight days with the truck to take us down again.

The forest above was thin and parched. It had obviously suffered from the same drought as the plains below. There were pencil-cedar trees, Podocarpus and clumps of bamboo, but none of them attained the size that we had found on the Aberdares. A few black-and-white Colobus monkeys crashed and jumped about among the tree tops, and over us flew a flock of small grey and red parrots. There were also two kinds of pigeon, one of them quite large, but they were reported not to be good eating owing to the Podocarpus berries on which they fed.

Our second camp was made at the top of the forest where the open moorland began. It was very dry here, and there were no arborescent senecios or giant lobelias. Both of them are water-lovers. In their place was a scrub of Protea, a small bushy plant with gigantic creamy flower-heads, pushing up from the top of the branches like an egg out of the eggcup.

Commander Hook told us that the mountain plateau had been swept with fire a few years before. Yet still it was black and charred as if the fire had been only a few weeks ago. The rainfall on this end must be very slight. We had perfect weather, which was very lucky for us, since the tent with which we had been supplied had already several holes and did not appear as if it would be able to stand up well to a severe storm.

As we crossed the dry land above the second camp, a speck of brilliant green on the side of a ravine attracted me. The small telescope confirmed that it might be the big leaves of a giant groundsel, the first of the mountain. Soon I was speeding towards it, telling Hancock and his party to go on, saying that I would rejoin him in a quarter of an hour. But the big leaves were on the other side of the ravine, and here the vegetation turned into a thick scrub almost breast high, through which I had to battle and jump my way.

All the plants on this end of the mountain seemed to be concentrated in the ravines. At last I reached the bottom, where I found a little stream. It was a most delightful place. The stream fell over a miniature waterfall into a dark shady pool, on the bank was real green grass and rushes, dotted with pink orchids, while on the further bank a group of the giant groundsels arched over the water. On a rock in the centre of the waterfall grew a cascade of beautiful pink balsams.

In a glade there we found the wonderful blue delphinium, known as *D. macrocentrum*. I do not know of any other plant which attains quite the same subtle and electric shade of blue. It seems to combine the clearness and etherealness of the sky at sunset with a touch of green, and also the more vivid, more chemical tone of a solution of copper sulphate. It is distant and elusive in one glance, yet near, electric and vivid in another.

It was an hour and a half before I rejoined Hancock. I found him resting beside a small red survey flag, which some former party had set up. A few men had come up to him, but the majority were still behind.

We hoped to make our next camp near a rocky mass called Cæsar's Seat, where Commander Hook had reported there was a rock shelter under which the porters could sleep. But the men were finding the going heavy and we had to look out for a camp site earlier. We found out then that they were not really accustomed to carrying loads on the mountain, but usually worked on the farm in Nanyuki. They did not carry on the head as do the Uganda tribes, but with a strap strung round their forehead and shoulders.

A good camp site was found in a little valley about two miles below Cæsar's Seat. Beside us a little stream flowed, behind us was a big grey rock and a clump of scarlet gladioli. It was perfectly sheltered, so much, indeed, that the valley was difficult to find from the moorland around until one was actually standing on the brink of it. Some of the ground was swampy, and here the rosettes of the little *Senecio brassica* were freely sprinkled, white like cabbages with the hoar frost on them, and a cabbage covered with hoar forest is, in my opinion, a beautiful thing. Their spikes of yellow flowers and silvery stems were also attractive, and these dwarf plants had not the grotesqueness of the other members of the race, which formed great trunks. Above us Cæsar's Seat dominated the horizon, and away to the south were the snow peaks clearly visible most of the time. Whether this curious shaped mass is named after the great Julius Cæsar or after César, one of Mackinder's guides on the mountain, I do not know. As far as we could gather, much of the survey of this end of the mountain was still incomplete, or at least unpublished. The more usual route ascended the southern flanks.

In the afternoon I set out alone to visit Cæsar's Seat. This was like a great round table of rock stuck down on the mountain side. But it was so vast that its apparent nearness proved deceptive. It was nearly five o'clock before I reached it, but still an hour of daylight remained. No sign of a rock shelter could be found, nor was there any sign of the lake which Commander Hook had called 'The Nameless Lake', and which he had stated to be near. Its name, 'The Nameless Lake', only made us all the more anxious to find it, but we never succeeded. The valley with the camp was so perfectly hidden that I missed my way coming down, although all the country was open, and found myself wandering in search of the camp when darkness came down. It is an unpleasant feeling to be lost in the dark on a mountain, even though the camp is near, and I was very glad when I heard a whistle in answer to mine and so was able to guide myself back.

In the evening we sat round a great fire, or joined the Makerere boys at the fire they had made. They were very charming, and I quickly felt at my ease with them and found myself thinking of them as four English school-boys. They talked good English and had plenty to say, being full of interesting information about their life and country and asking many questions about life in England. I was able also to appreciate the keenness and inquisitive intelligence with which they applied themselves to learning about the plants and animals of the mountain.

It is often asserted against 'African' students that they lose the use of their hands as soon as they grasp a small amount of book learning. We did not find this so, and these four were certainly the most handy and useful of the Africans of the party when we made camp. They always seemed able to get their fire blazing before anyone else, and frequently then came over to help the Kikuyu boy and show him how it should be done. They seemed always smiling and always ready to help in every possible way, not excluding such tasks as should have fallen to the boys and porters.

The remainder of the safari seemed extremely ill-adapted to the mountain, but the cook undoubtedly was the greatest joke among us. It seemed that he did not know how to cook at all, and investigation showed that in the hotel he had only been a kitchen boy. Still, even for a kitchen boy he seemed phenomenally lethargic and dense in mind. One day he made some sandwiches for us. When we came to undo them we found that he had failed to put anything inside them, the butter he had put on the outside. Hancock and Semwanga patiently tried to teach him something, and towards the end of the safari he had learnt a little, but terribly little. Indeed, in some cases the educator of the African may well despair.

The porters were tired and sulky, quite unlike those we had had on any other mountain, although our moves had been extremely short, much shorter than the stages on Mt. Elgon.

We were anxious to make another camp higher up in the valley beyond Cæsar's Seat, whence we could reach the snows, but they flatly refused to go up any further. The boys could understand something of their talk and told us that they were frightened of the spirits which they felt dwelt on the mountain. As far as we could gather, one man had seen a spirit or had a warning dream and had communicated it to the others. Semwanga said he thought that they felt that the spirit of the God or Gods walked on Mt. Kenya. More than that I cannot say. It would indeed be a rash European who tried to tell definitely of such things without a very long experience of the country and a very complete sympathy and understanding with the people and their language. Perhaps it would be well if more of the tutors at African colleges took the opportunity of taking a holiday with some of the pupils and sitting round the same camp fire. There are fewer better ways of gaining a greater sympathy with their desires and their minds.

Since we were unable to establish a higher camp, we decided to make two expeditions with the pony as far up the mountain as we could get in one day. Hancock and Adrian went the first day and returned just before dark, reporting a good view of the main peaks, but that they had still been some distance off from them. The following day I went, accompanied again by Adrian and also by the four African boys. The pony proved useless when we came to a steep ravine quite early in the day and I had to send it back in charge of one of the Kikuyu boys, giving directions that he should bring it up the valley running from Cæsar's Seat towards the peaks to meet me in the evening. The snows were nearly always in view, but a seemingly endless succession of rounded grassy ridges seemed to separate us. At last we reached the top of the final one, about 14,000 feet, and looked across a broad valley, dotted with senecios, on to the snow peaks. I think it must have been the Mackinder valley. The peaks stood up almost sheer for over a thousand feet and we were able to recognize the extreme difficulty of their ascent. In spite of repeated attempts, the summit has only twice been reached, once by Sir Halford Mackinder and his Swiss guides in 1899, and then in 1927 by a party consisting of Mr. Eric Shipton, Mr. Wynn Harris and Mr. George Sommerfelt. Of the actual summits Batian and Nelion, the former is the higher by a few feet, attaining 17,040 feet. Between them is a dip which has been named 'The Gate of Mist'. A little way below the summit hangs the Diamond Glacier, which Mackinder reports as being of 'adamantine hardness'. Although it is only a hundred feet wide, it took him and his two guides three hours to cut steps and cross it. They say that they had in their estimates allowed twenty minutes for it.

The snow line was higher than we had expected. Probably owing to the drought on the mountain there had been no fresh snow recently. The boys were very anxious to feel and handle snow. They had, naturally, never done so in their lives. But it seemed impossible to reach the snow that day and then return to the camp, and we had to give up the project, content with a really magnificent view. Besides, both the boys and ourselves had begun slightly to feel the effects of the altitude. Afterwards one of the boys confessed to me that they had thought for a time that they were going to die. The vegetation here was sparse and the ground was chiefly covered with stones and rocks. Among them still grew the giant groundsels and lobelias. There were particularly magnificent stands of *Lobelia Telekii*, the great petrified woolly bear named after Count Teleki, the explorer. They suggested for us 'family life on Mt. Kenya'. There were two in particular which amused us, a tall one and a short one side by side. From a little distance they looked like two figures out for a walk, a tall man and his short wife. Then suddenly they had come over the crest into sight of the snow peaks and had stood there gazing at them petrified with surprise. There was also here the skull of a buffalo, showing how high up the mountain they may wander. What evil chance had brought it to die of hunger or cold up here?

Botanically the mountain was disappointing, being so very dry; probably the other sides would have been much richer. After this we returned quickly to camp, and by successive camps down to the glade where Commander Hook picked us up and laughed at our account of the safari, many parts of which by now almost resembled a drawing by Heath Robinson. On the way down two pictures remain in my mind: Kintu, one of the Makerere boys, descending the mountain with three empty debies slung on a pole over his shoulder. He shall have music wherever he goes was perforce true of him. 'Clatter, clatter', his approach could be heard a mile off. The other picture was the Kikuyu boys trying to load the tent on to the pony, slung in two loads on to each flank. They were singularly futile at it. One man attempted to blind the pony with a blanket, while another held him, and yet two more hoisted up the yoke with the loads. Then one of the boys would stick a pole of the bundle too near his flanks, and he would shy, scattering most of the boys and leaving the loads on the ground. Finally, in kindness to the unfortunate pony, we intervened and managed to get the loads put on more dexterously.

Our last evening at the highest camp was glorified by a dance of the porters in a ring around their fire, joyous at the thought that the coldest part was now over and that we were coming down. They jumped in the air, they circled the fire, they wriggled their bodies, chanting all the while, in the slow steady rhythm of Africa, which wanders on, so bewitchingly full of curves, but without angles, seemingly without beginning or end. Yet there was life, vital life, in every throbbing note of it as they danced, pagan-like, around the fire.

Semwanga entertained the whole party with a conjuring entertainment for our last night on the mountain. It was a very fine entertainment too. The tricks were apparently due to sleight of hand, and were similar or parallel to many European tricks, but he was extremely apt with them and nearly always managed to deceive me. There was one trick in particular which I could not master, in which he seemed to bang the palm of his hand down flat on the edge of a sharp knife several times, yet he never hurt himself in any way. He had mastered the patter of an entertainer marvellously, and being no longer at all shy of us he gave it out with great gusto. I have seldom seen better tricks on an English stage, and we had to confess him easily our master in this respect.

The companionship of these four Makerere boys is undoubtedly the memory that remains with me most powerfully of Kenya Mountain, and will remain long after the comical and inefficient side of the safari has faded.

On our return through Nairobi we spent a night in an hotel, and in the morning an hour in the famous Coryndon Museum. This is an excellent institution, and as alive as any museum I have seen recently. The only pity seemed to be that the museum is at Nairobi, while the college and future university of East Africa is at Kampala.

CHAPTER IX

BLUE WATER LILIES

Slowly we glide out through a long lane of water cut through the papyrus thicket into Lake Kioga, where the blue water lilies cover the surface with a far-stretching shimmer of green and blue.

Our craft is one of the long dugout canoes, and we perch either in the bows with camera ready or recline in the centre. We are searching in particular for the rare whale-headed stork who boasts the proud title of *Balaeniceps rex*. The swamps of Lake Kioga are one of his last haunts. It is really only courtesy which dignifies Kioga with the name of lake. All of it is shallow, and much is merely a great swamp.

The bird life is extremely rich, but for a long time we could not sight one of the whale-headed storks. Hither and thither we went, until finally Hancock sighted a small grey hump almost hidden by a clump of papyrus in the distance. It was *Balaeniceps*. He stayed motionless until we approached quite close, brooding as a solitary monarch over his estate. He is a large pale blue grey bird, and stands four feet or more from the ground. His head is swollen like the head of a hammer or like the head of a whalebone whale, and this has earned for him his name of whale-headed stork. His beak has a small hook at the end and he lives on fish. These are very plentiful in Lake Kioga. We were able to approach quite close, gliding forward with infinitesimal speed until the camera clicked and he made off. Luckily he was a very heavy bird and only flew about a hundred yards at a time, and then alighted in another tuft of papyrus. We were able to follow him up and try another photograph. I longed, though, for a silent shutter. My beautiful Soho reflex was out of order, and instead I had borrowed an old reflex whose shutter made a noise rather like a sack of coals falling on to a glass roof, a definite disadvantage for Nature photography. The best method of obtaining photographs would undoubtedly be to find a nest and build a hide near it. He nests on shore, but none of the lake men we met knew of a nest or remembered ever having seen one. Alternatively, good photographs could, I am sure, be obtained with a silent camera and a moderate telephoto. A high-powered telephoto is almost impossible to use from a canoe, since a tripod is necessary to get decent results. Some camouflage on the bows in the form of papyrus and reeds would, I think, be a help, and the paddlers must be trained to glide infinitesimally slowly and noiselessly towards the bird. The Africans will nearly always enter into the fun of it and help all they can, but absolute silence is not natural to them for any length and must therefore be carefully impressed.

The *Balaeniceps* is most strictly preserved, and at any rate we had no desire to shoot, but only to watch and photograph his poses and flight. With his swollen and distorted head he seemed a monstrous and fantastic creature, almost a survival from another age. Africa seems to be full of these anachronisms, these fascinating 'giants'. It is not only on the mountains that they occur.

An even greater bird was the goliath heron, *Typhon goliath*, a beautiful slim grey figure which stood on a tuft of rushes or waded slowly through the shallow water. He would stand poised and quite motionless, seemingly for hours, yet always alert and ready to make a lightning stab with his long beak when a fish came near. He was quite five feet in height and sometimes nearer six. He was very common, but we never tired of watching his slow graceful movements and marvelling at his beautiful poise. Compared to him, *Balaeniceps* was a heavy lout of a bird.

Pelicans were also common and looked delightful sailing majestically among the blue water lilies. With their huge beaks and little saucy round eyes they have a rare comical charm. When they flew there was a great clatter and flurry, but finally the great bird took to the air and flew away with at least a modicum of grace.

Black cormorants and darters are present in innumerable quantities, and it is possible to get quite close sometimes, particularly to the young ones, which sit stupidly on a clump of rushes till the boat is almost on top of them, stretching their long necks first this way, then that, in earnest enquiry, like a goose.

Over the water lilies run the lily trotters, small tern-like birds with long legs and enormously long toes, enlarged so as to spread the weight over the water lily leaf, whose buoyancy supports them. They never seem to fall through the leaves into the water or allow their rafts to sink under them as they hop about from leaf to leaf and poke their beaks in the water for food. Shooting their heads forward on their graceful necks they would cry out a shrill warning of our approach, which echoed across the lake, being passed from bird to bird. Then there are the black-and-white kingfishers which hover over the water with rapidly pulsating wings until they suddenly descend in a swift dive after a fish. Quite often they catch it, too. They are larger than the common English species, but they do not gleam with his rich iridescent blue. They are, indeed, almost dowdy in their barred coats of black and white. There is, however, also a little blue kingfisher with an orange breast, gleaming terrifically bright.

There are also many other fine birds, including the curious open bill stork and various kinds of duck which may be shot during certain seasons.

At the edge of the lake grow the ambatch trees, and dangling on their branches are the nests of the weaver birds, maybe fifty in one tree, a twittering, quivering mass. Each nest is truly a house. It is round, like an Eskimo igloo, like a great woolly ball which has been hollowed out. In the side is a hole through which the bird enters, and sometimes the suspicion of a ledge on which he can perch. The whole is little larger than a tennis ball, and the bird is the size of a small sparrow. For comfort and warmth such a nest would seem to represent a great improvement on the open nest. Yet it is only in the tropics that such hanging ball nests are found, where the nights are warm and no such extra protection would appear to be needed. They are also limited to small birds.

The lake is glorious. The water is very clear and we can see down to the bottom, where little fish play among the water weeds. It is wholly attractive in colour and fairylike in form. Under the water lily leaves there are very dark shadows contrasting with the green shininess of the leaves, over which drops of water run like quicksilver, splitting and joining in a merry antic, and ever trying to find their way back again to the water below. The blue flowers are not born nestling in the water as in the English species. They stand proudly six or eight inches above it. Among them are a few pink flowers and some big white ones, probably the true *Nymphœa lotus*, and maybe the Egyptian lotus sacred to Isis. Beautiful though it is, this plant cannot compare with the sacred bean, *Nelumbium speciosum*, the lotus figured and revered by the Chinese, a superb plant, without equal in the whole plant world. It also grows in marshes and even out of mud. In the black mud of the lake these blue water lilies conceal long fat tubers, which the Africans sometimes pull up and eat. This is not, though, the source of the lotus eaters of Greek mythology. This lotus is yet another plant, a shrub named *Zisyphus*. The water lilies form a fringe twenty to fifty yards wide all round the edge of the lake and around every island, while in shallow parts there are acres, and even square miles, veritable seas, covered with them. As the sun comes out all the flowers open. When the sun goes in all the flowers close. The scent is delicious and the silence is broken only by the slight buzz of the bees among the flowers, and the whistling of the breeze which always seems to sweep over the lake. It is delicate, like the whispering murmurs of the sea in a shell held up to the ear.

As we pass among them sometimes we lean out and pull a flower. It comes away with a yard or two of green stem, which lies curling in the shadow at the bottom of the boat. At the edge of the lake men can be seen wading in and out, tending the fish traps, which are like great conical baskets with openings on the lobster pot principle.

Around there are low hills and blue sky with great rolling white clouds, which are reflected in the water among the lilies. There is little sound except the gentle tap of the water on the bows of the canoe and the splash of the paddles. It is very perfect peace. Even that sound ceases as we moor up to a clump of papyrus. Somerville paints a picture from one end while I dally with a piece of canvas and a brush at the other, to the considerable detriment of the canvas. In the middle of the boat Ford and Hancock slumber. Dark storm clouds approach over the sky, and against them the papyrus stands out like a feathery ball of green, intense and brilliant and with every strand visible. The cloud comes nearer. Hancock has brought the only mackintosh, and he cannily bargains with Somerville to lend it to him against the gift of a picture. We land on the island near and clamber up the only small hill, to discover that it is a considerably larger island than we had realized. Our chief paddler guides us along a small path through the fringing acacias and we emerge by a little village, beating the rain to a hut by a very short head. The lady of the house receives us kindly and gives us shelter, yet she still remains aloof, timid and shy. These people on the islands are not quite the same tribe as the people on the mainland. They seem more primitive and shy.

The papyrus is a wonderful plant. Around the edges of the lake it forms thickets ten feet high, bound together with twining plants and ferns, a swaying, treacherous, semi-floating mass. Hidden amongst it are all manner of choice little flowers, but the getting of them is no light job. The tufts of papyrus are generally separated by channels of water, although these are often veiled by the mass of dead and decaying vegetation which carpets the swamp. The tussocks are not firm, but wobbly like a sponge, which seems to delight to cast one off into the water and the mud. Among them grows a Hibiscus with fine yellow flowers like a hollyhock, but painfully prickly stems. The papyrus swamp is a jungle of luxuriant growth through which it is necessary to hack and cut a way. As one moves, the papyrus closes over one's head and there is a close resemblance to some new and strange kind of forest. It would be easy to get lost in such a mass of vegetation, since it is necessary to keep on moving practically all the time to prevent oneself sinking through.

When seen alone, as on a small island where only two or three heads stand up outlined against a light sky or a dark stormcloud, then, indeed, the papyrus is superb. Its head is like a great Catherine-wheel of green, yet, albeit, it is feathery and delicate like the outline of plants in some Chinese or Japanese painting. It has so much of the lightness and charm of the bamboo as it waves in the wind that I am sure it would have been a favourite subject for their painters if it had grown in China or Japan.

The stem is long and triangular. The ancient Egyptians used it extensively for making writing paper which they called papyrus. They used to cut the stem in slices and then weave these together. Some of the Uganda peoples now use the papyrus as rafts, binding the stems together in bundles. It can also be used for thatching. There are several thousands of square miles of this papyrus swamp in Uganda and in the Sudd region of the Southern Sudan. It is possible that in the future these may prove one of their country's most valuable assets, although at the moment they are regarded merely as so much waste land. Papyrus is one of the fastest growing and most luxuriant of all plants. In one year's growth it will reach a height of eight to ten feet. As far as is known at present it will regenerate if cut annually. Whether, if systematically cut every year, it would continue to regenerate is not known: only experiment would give us that knowledge. On Wicken Fen, close to Cambridge, the mixed sedge is cut every four years for thatching, and regenerates well, but then growth in Cambridge is very much slower than growth in East Africa. It is possible that it would be necessary to restrict cutting to once every two years. It is unlikely that more frequent cutting would be desired although it might be possible.

The extent of the supply of timber for the wood-pulp used in the manufacture of paper and the deposits of oil fuel have recently caused much controversy and anxiety. Timber does regenerate itself, but we are cutting faster than regeneration takes place; living, or, rather, writing, on our capital. Every year the output of the press and the publishers becomes greater. Manifestly there is over-production both of books and newspapers, but no halt in their production seems likely. The supplies of oil are not inexhaustible, and experts have frequently stated that we are using them up both wastefully and rapidly. Oil does not regenerate itself. It is a heritage from the past, and has taken many thousands, or even hundreds of thousands, of years to form.

It is possible to make both paper pulp and power alcohol from papyrus. Laboratory experiments have shown this; nevertheless, experiments on a much larger scale would be necessary prior to any exploitation scheme. The present low price of petrol and wood-pulp would be likely to defeat any such project at the present moment with regard to the export market, but in the near future it is not inconceivable that natural grass vegetation may become our chief source of fuel and pulp. It is probable that there is no grass, rush or reed, which grows faster than papyrus.

Undoubtedly there are certain difficulties, but these are probably not very severe. The greatest difficulties would arise in connection with harvesting. There is little or no native population in the swamps, and they are regarded as unhealthy. Cutting would have, therefore, to be done chiefly by machinery. But the papyrus swamp will not bear the weight of any heavy machine. It would be likely to sink through into the mud, and there it would remain for a future age to excavate, if, indeed, a future age so far off is likely to have any interest in archæology; but perhaps then everything will be so perfect and they will have so much leisure that there will be nothing much else to do than to investigate the curious customs of the past. Still, we are wandering again. Some of the papyrus could be harvested from the edge of clear channels, but these would always be liable to blocking with floating islands of papyrus, and even so the papyrus reached would only be a very small percentage of the total. It seems unlikely, though, that such a mechanical difficulty could not be overcome by distributing the weight over a large surface, and that then some form of very light railway carrying cutters and binders would not be able to be constructed.

There is an antelope called the situtunga which lives in the papyrus swamps. He is the only large mammal to do so. He used to be common, but now is becoming scarcer owing to hunting. We never saw one actually in the papyrus, but were lucky enough to see a tame one in the game warden's garden at Entebbe. He is a shy and delicate looking beast. His hooves are so enlarged that he does not sink straight through the papyrus tufts as would an ordinary antelope. For our machinery we would obviously have to follow his example and distribute the weight over a large base.

Any utilization scheme would undoubtedly need the establishment of factories on the spot, since transport to the coast would be prohibitive on anything except the finished article. The papyrus itself could probably be made to supply the motive power for the factory. There are ample sites in Uganda, and there is reputed to be a suitable site on a hill in the middle of the Sudd region of the Sudan. It would be probable that any scheme would start by catering for local demand rather than export. In East Africa petrol is far more expensive than in England owing to the high cost of transport from the coast. At present it is two shillings and fifty cents per gallon in Nairobi, but in regions further inland it rises to three shillings and fifty cents, and even higher. Then in Africa distances are great, roads comparatively empty and sometimes rough. High-powered cars, with consequent high petrol consumption, are desirable, if not essential, for work outside the towns.

However, I have said enough about the papyrus and must resume the story of our wanderings on the lake. As we crossed a broad open patch of water on our way home, the paddlers began to sing and chant, dipping in their paddles in time to the music. 'What are they singing about?' I asked. Hancock translated for our curiosity. He said: 'We are paddling very fast, we are paddling very fast, for we are carrying great Bwanas over the water. We are paddling very fast,' a flattering, though somewhat euphemistic and fallacious statement in both respects. Still, the African is somewhat like the proverbial Irishman, in that he will generally say what he thinks will give most pleasure rather than bothering about the truth. The canoes are dugouts made from a single great tree-trunk by burning and gouging out the centre, but they are not built for any speed. The prows are blunt and almost rectangular, being only slightly curved upwards to pass among the rushes and water lilies. These range from the small single-seater to the larger family canoe, and finally the omnibus canoe which serves as a ferry. Generally they brought out the omnibus for us.

On Lake Victoria the canoes made by the Baganda tribe are more elaborate, having often a double layer of planks fixed as wash-strakes above the dugout, which serves as keel and base. In addition they have an upturned false prow, which generally consists of a separate piece of wood fitted on horizontally and turning up at right angles from the water towards the end. Sometimes this is decorated with carving and gives the boats a much more distinguished appearance, a step in the direction of the Viking canoe with carved figurehead. Lake Victoria is renowned for its sudden and violent storms, and it is a serious matter for any canoe caught in one of these far from land. We must think of Lake Victoria as an inland sea, comparable in size to the great lakes of North America. Yet it is very shallow. The waves are generally of the short, choppy type, coming very close together. This type is common on large expanses of shallow water. Undoubtedly these false prows do help the boats to ride better across these waves.

Sailing is popular among the Europeans stationed at Entebbe and Kampala, and there are several small boats, but they cannot venture very far out for fear of the sudden storms. An African canoe with a sail and outriggers fitted is reputed to be the fastest of all. The coast is beautiful, indented with little bays and fringed with papyrus and palms. On the horizon are many little islands. Bathing is dangerous in most places along the beach because of the crocodiles, but it is safe and very pleasant from a boat about a mile from shore. Apparently the crocodiles do not cross the open water much, but keep to the shallow water near the edge of the lake.

It is interesting to contrast the canoes made by the African of these great inland waters with those made by the Borneo peoples, for whom there are no roads but rivers. These are far finer products, being often one of the most valued possessions of a 'longhouse', and, maybe, shaped for racing. They are very long and narrow, yet some hold fifty or even a hundred men. Their prows are sharp and curved so that they are raised above the water. There is occasionally a carved figurehead, but more often not. Often one man sits right up in the bows cross-legged like a figurehead, giving the time to the paddlers, and sometimes dashing in his paddle with a lightning stroke to keep the boat off the rocks in a rapid. Now that head-hunting as a pastime and an impetus to young warriors is largely a thing of the past, much of their energy goes into racing their canoes. Each year a big regatta is held in which the 'longhouses' race against each other. It is one of the great functions of the year. Many boats have recorded a time almost approximating to that of a university crew. Their rivers are fast-flowing and liable to torrential floods and full of rapids, so that they test a boat to the full. The people also have been great fighters and are naturally alert and intelligent.

It is interesting to speculate what kind of a canoe the East Africans might have produced if they had had to contend with fast-flowing rivers instead of great lakes. Several writers have suggested that the East African lake canoe is derived from the more eastern peoples through the Zanzibar and Arab traders of the Middle Ages, who undoubtedly penetrated into Uganda. Such is the argument brought forward by 'the Diffusion of Culture' school, and undoubtedly the process has played a large part in the lives and cultures of primitive peoples. Still, the majority of peoples accept the occurrence of what they are pleased to call 'original sin' in children, so why should we not accept the idea of an original and perhaps slightly parallel evolution of a canoe in response to the universal desire for crossing the water. Every primitive people must have noticed for themselves that a piece of wood floated and that it would support a weight, such as a bird. From there it would be a short step for such an amphibious race to find out that a large enough piece would support a man.

Dr. and Mrs. Worthington, in their excellent book on the *Inland Waters of Africa*, have devoted a whole chapter to the evolution of the East African canoe, and have traced its development in such a clear and complete way that it is unnecessary for me to say much more on the same ground. They came to the conclusion that the Baganda canoes were derived from the dugout canoes, and that the whole was indigenous to Africa, a conclusion with which I am in agreement.

There are practically no large sporting fish in Lake Victoria, but below the Ripon Falls, at Jinja, where the young Nile leaves the lake, there are great barbel which can be seen jumping into the waterfall to try and get up, but always falling back. In the corner of the falls, though, is a lesser trickle and a few seem to ascend here, but no one reports seeing one ascend successfully in the main fall where they mostly try. They fall an easy prey to the rod and fisherman's spoon, and good sport can be enjoyed just below the falls, the fish ranging up to twenty pounds or even more.

Into Lake Victoria flows the uttermost source of the Nile, the Kagera river; so the actual lake may almost be considered as a source. The Victoria Nile is its only outlet, but the amount of water flowing over the Falls is very slight in comparison to the area of the lake. Much is lost by evaporation over the surface. Only a slight lowering of the level of the lake would mean that no water would escape into the Nile. There is considerable support for the theory that Africa is entering on a dry interpluvial cycle, and that the climate is slowly becoming drier rather than damper. If so, this source of the Nile might be closed. Such an event, though, is not likely to come into the very near future. It is, however, definitely a possibility of the future. Another possibility, but a very remote one, is an upheaval corresponding to the rift movements, which might leave Lake Victoria to drain southwards and westwards into the Congo system. Such a contingency, however, can hardly be discussed as it is so very remote. The loss of the water from the Victoria Nile would be most serious to the Sudan and to Egypt, since it is the most regular of the Nile sources, varying little with different seasons.

CHAPTER X

CROCODILES AND FLAMINGOES

CROCODILES, crocodiles, crikey what a lot of crocodiles! In serried ranks they lie, rank upon rank, almost belly upon belly, covering the mud banks to the side of the river and gliding, loglike, through the water. The scene is the Victoria Nile in the stretch between Lake Albert and the Murchison Falls.

Lake Albert is rather different in formation from Lake Victoria. It lies at the bottom of a long narrow rock basin with the Congo hills to the west, Ruwenzori to the south, and the Uganda escarpment to the east. Its edges are hot and dry, brown and barren, with powdery dust as earth and very scanty thorn scrub. From the top of the escarpment the road winds down to the lake, lying a thousand feet below, a blue hazy mass, shimmering in the heat. On a clear day faintly blue on the far side can be seen the Congo hills. Around the edge lie the crocodiles. The Murchison Falls are now one of the sights of Uganda, and many parties visit them for the sake of seeing the abundant wild animals which occupy the game reserve, through which the river passes between Lake Albert and the Murchison Falls. It is also a sleeping sickness reserve, so there are no inhabitants to interfere with the game, and no one may land between the lake and the falls. By April the rest of the expedition had all sadly returned to England, one by one, and I was thinking of following their example. Meanwhile I was glad of the chance of going with Christopher Harris, a forest officer with whom I was then staying, up to the Falls. We were joined by another party from Kampala and set off late in the evening from Butiaba, the port on Lake Albert from which the trip up the Victoria Nile is begun. It is also from here that the journey down the Nile to Khartoum starts. The Victoria Nile enters Lake Albert and the White Nile leaves it, both at the north end and within a few miles of each other.

It was a glorious night as we steamed across the lake, which was absolutely calm. The vessel was a woodburner, and the funnel gave out a continuous stream of sparks and glowing splinters, lighting up the night in a never-ending shower of golden fireworks. It was a perfect setting and we sat in the bows watching, marvelling at the pattern of gold, more brilliant than any nocturne picture, until we gradually fell asleep. Behind us the crew slept, sprawling over the bulwarks and passages, so that whenever we moved we seemed to fall over some almost moribund dark corpse.

At dawn we reached the mouth of the river and disembarked into a smaller launch which was to take us up to the Falls and had been towed behind from Butiaba. The captain, an Indian, said that the water was very low and that the big launch could not go as usual.

The lower stretch of the river is papyrus fringed, and birds were the chief attraction. There were Ibis and goliath herons, and white-breasted fish eagles and many others. The fish eagle is a very fine bird. With his white breast he is conspicuous as he sits perched on a tree by the side of the river looking out for fish below. In size he is a little larger than the golden eagle. He is, however, a common bird, while the golden eagle is now very rare.

Our only regret was the speed of the launch, which carried us past before we had seen nearly enough. The papyrus lasted for several miles, and then we emerged into scrub savannah country with short grass and small acacia trees and other spinous plants. On both sides of the river this territory is a game reserve, and it must be one of the richest in animal life anywhere in Africa. Waterbuck and hartebeeste, and all manner of deer, were frequent. There was hardly a moment during which there was not some interesting creature in sight.

Hippo and crocodiles were so abundant that we became quite 'blasé' about them, only bothering when one came up very close to us. In some places the river was almost solid with them. Hippo basked on the sandbanks, just submerged at the edge of the river, and swam about with their heads half above water. The hippo is definitely one of the animals which benefit in appearance by being three-quarters submerged. He is far more like his nearest relative the pigs than any horse. On land he can move quite fast, although he is such a grotesque figure of fun with his vast body, his short legs, his dirty pink, hairless skin, and his monstrous head. When he opens his mouth to yawn it is like a great and mysterious cavern opening before one. In the water he submerges himself until only the top of his head is visible. Like points, his bulging nostrils and little ears stick up above the surface.

Most of the hippo were quite unmoved by our passage, but one beast, probably an old rogue male, took it into his head to charge at the boat, swimming very fast under water and followed by a great wave. However, he was not a very good judge of speed and always missed. Soon he was left completely behind.

The crocodiles lay along the banks in serried ranks, somnambulant in the sun. Some were great monsters which must have been quite twenty feet in length. Many were considerably larger than the famous Lutembe of Lake Victoria. They did not even appear to wake or blink one of their monster eyelids as we passed. Still, even asleep they had an appearance of villainy, so loglike and yet so potent.

Elephants were our especial hope, and on the way up to the falls we saw a fine solitary beast standing at the river's edge. On the way down we were even luckier, and saw a pair throwing water over each other and playing together like a pair of little boys or puppies. It was a magnificent spectacle. Another pair followed us along the bank in the bushes for some distance, and at intervals we saw their backs projecting above the scrub. They must indeed be very abundant in this region. Lion were also reported from the neighbourhood, but we did not see any. Unfortunately, the Indian captain was in a bad temper and would not go as slowly as we had hoped. So that we rushed past the elephants and were not able to secure any good photographs.

At the falls we had only a short time, but I was able to get up to the place where the whole of the Victoria Nile flows through a gorge only twenty feet wide. Someone has kindly placed a seat there where one can sit and meditate on the power of the foaming torrent which swept downwards through the gorge. The crocodiles were swimming about in the pool below the falls, moving slowly like driftwood, so that they would have attracted little attention if we had not known what they were. As long as he does not show his light-coloured belly the crocodile is probably the best camouflaged animal of all, and normally he keeps in positions where his colouring is most effective.

The boat grounded on a sandbank near the mouth of the river on the way back. Dusk found us all standing in two to three feet of water, heaving and pushing. Luckily no crocodiles came near. Perhaps the commotion, which was considerable, frightened them. The Indian captain excelled himself with the engine. While we shoved forward he would put the engine into reverse. While we shoved backwards he would put it into forward gear. Frequently he stopped it altogether. At last Harris had to take over the engine, the boat slid off the sandbank, and we all, dripping, climbed aboard. However, she ran on to another five minutes later. This time we got off more quickly and reached the big launch which was waiting at the mouth of the river. We steamed quickly back to Butiaba, having mostly changed our wet clothes for pyjamas and coats.

Lake Albert is renowned for the vast Nile perch taken there, some of which approach three hundred pounds. We spent several days trying to catch a big one but without any success. We joined forces with an English visitor to the neighbouring Lake Albert Hotel, a Colonel well accustomed to the art of fishing and with a cunning array of lures. However, nothing availed, and we only caught a few Nile perch of two to three pounds and some small tiger fish. These latter are beautiful fish, long and thin like a mackerel and gleaming like a bar of silver. Their teeth are sharp and pointed, and give them an aspect of great ferocity. On a light rod they will often provide good sport. They are also reputed to serve well as live bait for catching Nile perch. Unfortunately, they make poor eating, being coarse and rather muddy to taste. Along the shore we could see the African fishermen standing in about three feet of water and casting out long lines, but they didn't seem to catch much either.

The two methods of fishing most used by the Borneo peoples are not common in East Africa. They are the tuba fishing in which a part of the river is barricaded off and the fish stupefied by poison until they come and float helpless on the surface to be harpooned by the men and scooped up in nets by the women. It is not a method suitable to lake fishing but only to river fishing. The other fishing implement in Borneo which made a great impression on us was the chain net, which an expert would coil up beside him and then throw out so that it covered a large area. We tried this too, but were not nearly so successful, the net merely falling in a heap at our feet. In every country successful fishing is the game of the expert. The Borneo expert would not have been able to cast a salmon fly, although undoubtedly he could have learnt, for their hands were very subtle.

Lake Albert lies at the bottom of the Rift valley. All round is a high escarpment of dry and rather barren thorn scrub country. Every year it is burnt in a rather futile endeavour to provide fresh grass. Consequently there is no chance for any trees to colonize and grow, although not far off is the magnificent forest of the Budongo, one of the finest in Uganda and yielding a high percentage of good African mahogany. It is now systematically worked. Cutting, regeneration and planting are carried out according to plan, so that cutting cannot outrun growth but establishes a nice balance with it. No trees under a certain size may be cut, so that young timber is not wasted. From Harris's house the forest ran green right up to the horizon.

At Kibero, on the edge of Lake Albert, is an old salt works, to which we paid a visit one day, scrambling a thousand feet on a narrow path down the side of the Rift. Salt used to play a most important part in African economy. Now civilization brings extraneous supplies of salt and we found this salt works and village partly deserted. Every year, we were told, there are fewer workers. The salt bubbles up from the ground in the form of warm springs and the water is retained by an ingenious system of mud ramparts which give the appearance of an ancient city partly excavated. For a moment I thought that instead of a salt works we had made an archæological find, but in reality these mudworks are increased annually and are all quite recent.

The process of extraction is complicated. First the salt is concentrated in the sand between the ramparts by evaporation. Each family has its allotted area. The salt-bearing sand is then put into a pot with a small hole in the bottom. Hot water is run through this sand into a pot below, producing a solution of intensely salt water.

The salt is obtained from this by evaporation over fires in the corners of their huts. It is then sold in neat little baskets made from banana leaves. The prices are low, and we reckoned that a family could only gain a very meagre living in this way after they had paid the licence for the salt-working and their normal taxes.

All people need a small amount of salt, and civilized people, who can buy it at the grocer's for a few pence, do not often realize what a problem salt may be in the lives of more primitive peoples, living far from the sea. Now Africa is fast becoming civilized and European salts are common. Formerly the only two supplies in Uganda, a country twice the area of England and Wales, were those of Kibero and of the salt lake at Katwe at the south end of Ruwenzori. From Katwe a considerable amount was, and still is, exported to the Congo. We bought salt from there for the Ruwenzori expedition, a hundred-weight sack for a few shillings. It forms a necessary part of porters' rations.

Two other lakes must be mentioned: Lake Nakuru with its marvellous flock of flamingoes, which we visited on our way up country from Nairobi; and Lake Naivasha, where we fished for black bass. Both of these lakes lie at the foot of the great branch of the Rift valley which runs up through Kenya.

Thirty miles from Nairobi brought us to the edge of the Rift valley. This is one of the geological wonders of the world. At the edge we stopped, gazing enthralled at the view over the valley far below. It was so vast, so blue, seemingly so endless, that it was hard to realize it was a valley. The perfect cone of Longenot stood out clearly against a wonderful blue horizon. It cannot have been so very long ago that it was an active volcano. Craters like little eruptions dotted the plain, which seemed to us a little miniature world of blue and pink patchwork spread out for our delectation. In the foreground the slope was covered with candelabra Euphorbias and other exotic succulents representative of the dry country. Eagerly Ford and I scrambled about among the grey rocks which blended so harmoniously with the Indian red of the soil. Somerville drew a few lines and gazed, as only an artist gazes, out over the valley, seemingly lost in its beauty and immensity. A few olive-green trees, windswept and spindly, dotted the slope among the Euphorbias, while in the distance could be seen a group of goats tended by a few little black boys, snatching what they could from the very meagre lusciousness of the escarpment.

What wonderfully decorative things are these Euphorbias when their geometrical patterns stand up against a brilliant blue sky, maybe the only real patch of green in a dried-up brown landscape! In their richness of colour they are almost reminiscent of the deepness and dominating tone of our lone pine in winter. They can usually be seen at a great distance, and often grow singly. They are very characteristic of Africa and take the place that the Cacti take in the drier parts of America. How decorative an avenue of these trees would be! I heard tell of such an avenue once, but never actually saw one. Only, alas, so many people are afraid of their unusual form, and see in it not beauty but only grotesqueness. The Euphorbias are, to me, more truly African than any other tree we saw.[1]

Much of the country down below was very dry and had obviously suffered from the effects of soil erosion and the cutting down of such few trees as may once have

---

[1] Subsequent to the writing of this chapter I have been re-reading Dr. Julian Huxley's *Africa View*, and have noticed that he makes the same suggestion for an avenue of candelabra Euphorbia trees, possibly alternating with scarlet Flamboyantes. Such would undoubtedly be a great addition. In Uganda the scarlet Spathodea, or even Kirikiti, might be used since Flamboyantes are not common.

stood there. Soil erosion and the thoughtless destruction
of trees are among the most pressing problems confront-
ing Africa to-day. In many places nearly all the soil has
already been washed away, leaving bare furrows. Down
these the water rushes away to the sea, doing no good to
the land, since it is lost so quickly. Each time the water
carries with it as silt some of the precious soil. When the
soil is bare of trees it is defenceless before the power of
the water. Only roots can bind it together and hold it
back. In a large proportion of the country around Naivasha and Nakuru the vegetation was still open. There
were large patches where the grass had not closed over
the soil. The earth was like dust and looked almost useless
for the farmer. Lake Elmenteita was free of flamingoes
when we passed, but we found one at least of the famous
flocks on Lake Nakuru. Even from a distance they could
be seen as a pink fringe to the lake, long before the
individual birds could be distinguished. The red dust of
Kenya is very abundant and very penetrating. At
Nakuru we arrived about dusk literally covered with this
red powdery dust, wanting only a bath and a drink. Both
were easily and quickly obtained at the hotel there. In
the morning we set out to visit the flamingoes. We
approached through a marshy wood of acacias, flat-topped,
and branched like many-tiered umbrellas. Here the hippo
had evidently been wallowing. Normally, this animal
does not seem to harm people unless it happens to bump
right up against them. But we had heard tales in Nakuru
that only the night before a restless and maybe pugna-
cious hippo had strayed several miles from the lake up
to the town and had bitten off the arm of a child. So we
kept a good lookout. Down by the lake the hoof marks
were gigantic, but we did not meet any of the beasts
themselves that day. From the acacia wood we emerged
on to a bank of mud where we wallowed up to our knees
in an attempt to get near the birds and photograph them.

The stench of the mud was considerable, and we tried, though without much success, to pick our way among the hardest bits, jumping the channels. We were subsequently informed that this mud, of which there was nearly a quarter mile belt, was very invigorating and hygienic—due to the soda of which the lake is full. The lake was all hazy and very pale soft blue. Against it the pink flamingoes made a wonderful symphony of colour.

The birds rose in a glorious cloud when we got near. The sky became pink instead of blue. They seemed so numerous that it was impossible for them all to rise together. The air immediately above the lake was full, and some had to wait until the first birds had moved off a little way. They are so large that before rising each bird has to take a comical little run like an aeroplane taking off. In flight they look like gigantic pink crosses, tipped with black on the laterals. The head, legs, body, and upper surface of the wings are all pink, but the under part of the great wings, particularly near the tips, is dark. In flight they stretch both their legs and neck out straight.

The flamingo is an ungainly and rather grotesque bird. His legs are like two thin sticks about three feet long, while his neck is equally long and scraggy, twisting snakelike down to the water. He paddles perpetually in the shallow places with his long neck bent down and his fat beak resting on the mud. With this beak he sifts the water and mud, feeding, like the whale, on the small organisms so obtained. During feeding the beak is pointed backwards so that the bird looks through its own legs. There is hardly any sound, no raucous shrieks or hoglike grunts, but just a little murmuring noise made by the feeding flamingoes and the gentle lapping of the water. All is peaceful, until suddenly the birds rise. Then the sky is overfilled with a brief pandemonium.

The young birds are not pink like the adults, but a dirty white in colour. They walk about at the edge of the flock. I was able to approach quite close to one group of them while Ford and Somerville stood on a more solid piece of ground, laughing at my flounderings after a group of birds which never ran fast but always seemed to move just a little faster than I did. The results, photographically, did not justify the mud, but still I enjoyed it.

It was nearly midday before we had finished with the flamingoes, bathed again, and left Nakuru. Still, it was only a hundred miles to Eldoret. Cheerfully we stopped to collect plants by the roadside—a delightful yellow *Hypoxis* and an orange *Gladiolus*—not expecting a sudden storm or knowing the effect of Kenya rain on the roads. Then it came on to rain. The road quickly became a quagmire. From an average of nearly thirty miles an hour we dropped to less than five, skidding all the way from side to side in spite of our chains. Without them we could not have moved. Other cars were in the same state. There was a whole line of them skidding comically in drunken zigzags across the road in front of us. Frequently Ford and Somerville had to get out and push, or even shovel away a bit of bank in front. Perhaps they felt safer outside the car. It was bad enough to drive a skidding car over a morass, but it must be far more unpleasant to be a passenger.

Much of this part of Kenya consists of so-called black cotton soil, although no cotton is grown there. When wet this presents about the worst possible surface for cars. Many of the roads seem to be composed almost entirely of this soil. Uganda is more fortunate. She has many deposits of hard red murram, which makes an excellent surface for roads. These stretch like great red ribbons into the sunset. They are literally red, not merely an anæmic pink or yellow, but a good rich flaming vermilion red. I was told, also, that the Uganda roads were well engineered in the first place and that this has made an enormous difference.

The road steadily rises, and we had by now left behind the dry thorn scrub of Naivasha for the wide expanses of short grassland which form the Eldoret plateau. These rush away in far rolling downs to distant horizons. It is almost Sussex transported into Africa; a Sussex without its little old-world villages and friendly feeling, but a Sussex with an even greater sense of space and freedom. Perhaps this typifies one of the greatest attractions of Kenya.

It is noticeable that far fewer Africans are to be seen on the roads of Kenya than of Uganda. Long stretches pass without the sight of anyone or any signs of cultivation. Of the few Africans we do pass, hardly any seem to smile as do the majority in Uganda. Kenya does not seem such a happy place as Uganda. The great majority, of course, either live in the reserves or work on the big European estates. There are very few African peasant smallholders in the highlands of Kenya as there are in Uganda. The women of the Kikuyu tribe are magnificent in their ornaments. Round their necks, arms and legs are twisted long coils of bright wire, while from their ears dangle heavy earrings.

The Kikuyu dress largely in old skins, and certainly have not the same standard of cleanliness with regard to their clothes as the Baganda. These latter, indeed, are inclined to be fastidious. They would not sleep in the same hut as the Kikuyu, for, they said, 'The Kikuyu do smell so.' When I went into the hut I had to admit that there was some truth in the statement. Most of the Kenya settlers always refer in rather derogatory terms to their 'Kuks', and say that all the best of them remain in the reserves, and that only the riff-raff come to work on European estates. This is probably true to some extent.

The highlands of Kenya are very English in appearance with their great rolling downlands, yet one does not feel that it is a homely, a friendly, or even a rich landscape such as we are used to in England. It is bare, vast and uncompromising. The extent of the soil erosion is terrifying. It is far worse than in Uganda. Yet we saw few plantations of trees or signs that any measures had been taken to stem the drain of the precious soil away to the sea.

At Naivasha we spent several days before going up into the Aberdare Mountains, which are close. Naivasha town seemed very dry and desolate. However, we had planned to await the rest of the party at the hotel by the lakeside. This was a beautiful place with a garden full of bright flowers stretching right down to the lake. The lake was large, but not oceanic as Lake Victoria. It was bounded by low ranges of blue hills, for all the world like Scotland. In the lake there was fishing—black bass, but not trout so low, and an African ghillie. There was, however, a very Scottish monster in the lake. This was a large hippopotamus. The African ghillie was much afraid of it and would fill the boat with large stones to throw at it and keep it off. We saw him bobbing up and down in the distance, but he never molested us in any way.

The black bass did occur, but neither in any great size or number. We were told that they had been more plentiful last year, again a very common Scottish and English remark with regard to fishing.

In the middle of the lake was a small island. On it was a little hut. When we rowed round we were shocked to see a large notice board, 'Private, No landing'. So English and so unAfrican. But still it emphasized one of the worst traits of the English mind, a character which it is most undesirable to encourage in a new country.

A road has been built round the lake. One afternoon we made a circular tour. South of the lake, the other side from Naivasha town, is a very arid, low range of hills with grotesque spiny plants. Against the dust and sand zebra could be clearly seen, and ostriches racing along.

They hardly seem to run, but stride along like long-distance walkers, but so long are their legs that their ultimate speed is quite considerable. The gazelle hardly seemed to run either. They leaped and bounded across the road most gracefully, and their jumps were so long, their landing so light, that they gave the illusion of flying. The hills around Naivasha are burnt up, dark in some lights, and purple like the Highlands of Scotland, but they are never green like the hills of Ireland.

CHAPTER XI

TOWN LIFE IN UGANDA

AFTER my return from Africa many of my friends asked 'What is Uganda like?' and more particularly, 'What is Kampala, its capital, like?' There are so few resident white men in Uganda that people in England have not yet learnt much about the country. Well, Kampala is very like any suburban town dumped down in the middle of Africa. It is very sad, but that is the impression left strongly on our minds. There are the same rows of little houses with little front gardens. In this case they are tin-roofed bungalows. There is the same general appearance of overcrowded and haphazard mess, a rubbish heap, as one friend described it to me.

Of course, there are some fine new buildings, such as the New Law Courts, the Agricultural Laboratories and the Indian School, but they do not seem to bear any particular relation to the rest of the town.

It is, indeed, a sorry place, having the air of an overgrown camp become permanent, not a country village, and not a city. There is nothing consciously African about it and it does not represent the best that Europe can produce. In that way I think we have definitely fallen below the standard which, as guardians and guides to the African, we should have put before him. As builders in a comparatively new country we should surely endeavour to give an example and to leave a heritage of beauty, the very best that the age can produce. Kampala is the centre of an important African kingdom and should be a fine city. It is just as much a part of education to provide beautiful things for the student to live with and know as to teach him history or biology. In fact, many think that it has the greatest educational value.

Of course, money does enter into the matter to some extent, although the country did not appear to me to be very poor. But I am sure that it is not primarily a matter of money, but rather of orderly planning and forethought, combined with some artistic and creative vision. In fact, it is real culture which is needed, not the pseudo-civilization whose dominating interests are golf and gossip, bridge, and petty money affairs.

Kampala is built on seven hills. So was Rome. But there the resemblance, at present, ends.

On the two highest are the two cathedrals, which dominate the town. One is Protestant, the other Roman Catholic. Facing each other so obviously, almost vying with one another in an apparent effort to be grandest and highest, they are a distressing reminder of discord and friction, the competition for souls that disturbed the early history of white interest and missionary endeavour in the country. It is a great pity that by their position they strike this note of rivalry, for both really represent a very considerable achievement, and missionary endeavour undoubtedly has done very much for the country.

We attended a service in the Protestant cathedral on Namirembe, the hill of Peace. Three-quarters of the congregation was made up of Africans. There could be no doubt that the Africans really entered into the spirit of the service and that it represented a very real force in their lives. Many of the hymns and the sermon were in Luganda. The congregation was very large. Not only did they sing, chiefly in tune, but they would sway their whole bodies in a very ecstasy of worship. It is good to think that they have been able to carry over the swaying rhythm of the body, one of the most alive features of their old life, into their new beliefs.

Situated on two of the other hills were the official seats of Medicine, Mulago Hospital, and learning, Makerere College. On another stood the tomb of Kabaka

Mutesa. This was certainly the most impressive African building we saw. It was built after the style of a vast hut in the centre of a courtyard and surrounded by a stockade. The roof was enormous and was thatched with dark grass. The eaves came down to within a few feet of the ground and were supported by almost black poles. From the eaves it mounted in a somewhat irregular curve to an apical point formed in the thatch over fifty feet above the ground. Inside it was dark. When our eyes became accustomed to the gloom, we saw a double row of dark wooden pillars reaching up to the roof, forming an aisle as in some ancient church. The whole seemed like some perfect miniature of a cathedral. Here we found the atmosphere and dignity which was lacking in the rest of the town. At the end of the building, as it were an altar, the late Kabaka's spears were grouped, pointing upwards to the roof and providing the only touch of strong colour in the building. Some of these were of exquisite workmanship and must have been very old. Placed on the floor in front of these spears was a very fine leopard's skin. The whole effect was very simple and for that reason most impressive.

From the cathedral we crossed a little valley on to the Makerere hill. Here was the East African Interterritorial College and the offices of the Department of Education. One of the most striking features of Makerere is the magnificent heronry of black-headed herons on a tree beside the road. The tree is very ancient and large, and many of its branches are pendulous. A colony of weaver birds share it with the herons, and on the ends of the pendent branches their little ball-like nests sway in the breeze. The herons live only on the top of the tree and there build their great uncouth nests of crossed twigs. These birds can always be seen silhouetted against the sky, standing motionless on long stilt-like legs with beaks half outstretched or else preening themselves in all manner of sinuous curves. It is rare to see fewer than twenty of the birds there, and generally there are considerably more. They are quite oblivious of passing traffic. In old times a market was held under the tree. The market is now held at the crossroads below, but still keeps the old name.

From here a dusty road leads into the town. Practically all the European shops and the Post Office are contained in one long straggling street, an irregular series of white concrete, wood, and corrugated iron. Every shape and style of building is here excepting only one in good modern or African style. A little away from this road there is an excellent bookshop now under the auspices of the C.M.S., and well patronised by the Africans as well as by the Europeans and Indians, altogether a valuable and most laudable venture. Below this road is another street of crowded Indian shops, where things are considerably cheaper. They are mostly wooden and ramshackle, and are stocked with every small thing conceivable. It is noticeable that there is no Woolworths, although such a shop seems most eminently suited to the African needs at the present moment and would be likely to do an enormous business. Of course, the Indian, to a certain extent, fulfils this need, but largely at his own prices.

The most interesting thing about Kampala is the kaleidoscope of African life to be found in the streets. Look at this fine Buick car approaching. Surely it must belong to some rich traveller or some high official. But, as likely as not, it is an African who steps out while his dark-skinned chauffeur holds the door. He is dressed, maybe, immaculately in a European lounge suit, or yet he may still wear the long white kansu introduced by the Arabs. As a dress it is dignified and stately. When an African member of the administration or Kabaka's council appears in public, as on the platform at a school speech day, I noticed that he always wore a white kansu.

Among the Baganda, perhaps alone of the African tribes, there exist landlords, and many of these have grown quite rich from the cultivation of cotton for export. This system apparently was not indigenous among them, but was due to the action of early English administrators who confirmed everyone in titles for any land they seemed to control at the moment, and some chiefs were confirmed as owners of large tracts which they formerly had only held as part of the tribal ground. However, Uganda is thinly populated, and I doubt whether much harm has been done. The occurrence among the population of some wealthy Africans may be a great help to the country. As usual in Africa, there is a preponderance of American cars, particularly Fords. British bicycles, however, hold the market and are proving a great boon to the African. Kampala has stacks of them. It is now every African boy's ambition to own a bicycle. There are few motor bicycles to be seen. Those few seem mostly to be owned and ridden by the missionary element; often they ride in full clerical attire, in spite of the heat and the dust.

During term time the Makerere boys are conspicuous figures in the town. Dressed, always immaculately, in white shorts, white shirt open at the neck, green stockings, green blazer with crest on the pocket, and green cap crested and tassled, they lord it in the town, even as top-hatted Etonians wander nobly through the streets of Eton and Windsor. It is a wise act that has excused the wearing of ties among them. Unlike Etonians, though, they have little money to spend, and so are probably not respected and favoured as are English public schoolboys.

Brilliant colour is added to the street scenes by the Baganda women, who wear, swathed gracefully round their bodies, the brightest printed cottons and silks. They seem particularly fond of scarlet, which contrasts wonderfully with their dark chocolate skins. Mostly tall and supremely well made, they walk with a luscious sinuous grace. A few adopt European costume, but the majority very wisely prefer the more African and definitely more suitable and graceful costumes made from cotton prints. Some carry gourds or water jars on their heads, and undoubtedly much of their carriage and grace are due to this. Everything in Uganda is carried on the head. Somerville reports that one day he saw a stately Muganda dame walking through Kampala with a single egg balanced on her head!

Buganda, with Kampala its capital, is probably the part of Africa, certainly East Africa, where the African has moved farthest along the path of civilization. This is almost entirely due to the early start of missionary endeavour in the country. Uganda has long been their pride, and they have concentrated their work there.

The Europeanization of the African in this district will astound the visitor who has travelled among more primitive tribes, but he cannot fail to note that they seem a cheerful and contented throng. Among the street crowds move the Indians, a few fine turbaned figures of Sikhs, but the majority are less spectacular in appearance, hailing from the central and southern provinces. There are also a number of Goans, who largely fill the posts of clerks in the shops and offices.

The Europeans are, for the most part, dressed smartly in ties, white suits and topees, but some in khaki shorts, open shirts and broad brimmed dusty double Terai hats. In the morning many of the wives of the European population may be seen shopping and housekeeping, exactly as they do in England. Unless she has some interest in African peoples or Natural History or some absorbing hobby, the European woman's life in Africa is likely to be rather an empty one, making her glad to devote time to petty housekeeping matters as in England. Her husband, if an official, will probably be away from her practically all day, and sometimes for longer stretches when he is sent on safari. The bachelors usually leave the petty shopping to their head boys.

Entebbe, where the higher officials live, is just over twenty miles off, on the shores of Lake Victoria. The road runs picturesquely through patches of bananas, little huts, and stretches of luxuriant forest in the valleys. The surface is excellent.

This time, however, we did not go straight through to Entebbe, but turned off a few miles short down a small track to the lake to see the famous crocodile Lutembe. Hancock was with us and he had brought some of his biology class from Makerere for a field lesson. They filled our two cars.

As soon as we approached the lake, the guardians of Lutembe came near and demanded large sums for fish to feed to her and for their services in fetching her. However, we knew that one shilling is their official reward, and this Hancock gave to one of his boys, telling him to make the necessary bargain.

This he did while the rest of us walked away a little and looked at a pair of crested cranes, which were prancing about prior to a scuffling fight. They are superbly beautiful and regal birds, and have been well chosen as the emblem and crest of Uganda. They walked up to one another daintily and gracefully, as if in a dance; then they seemed to give one peck at each other, rather a perfunctory peck, and retired in the same order. Finally, they both flew off together with a hen bird, who had been waiting inconspicuously by. In size they compare with a large heron, but are not quite so big as the goliath herons. Their body is a beautiful pearly silvery grey, while on their head is a magnificent erect golden-brown crest, which gives them their name. Their beaks are black, but the markings on the head and the fleshy wattles under the beak are red.

Suddenly a monstrous uproar attracts us back to Lutembe's rock. The keepers have agreed to call her for their traditional shilling and have begun to do so. They shriek as loudly as they can. They beat drums and old tin cans. There is a swirl in the water and Lutembe comes; right up to the bank she comes until nearly her whole body is out of the water. The keeper ventures within a few feet of her nose and makes her come even a little nearer for her piece of fish, which he holds out to her gingerly before putting it down a foot in front of her nose. With a sideways twist she opens her vast and villainous cavern of a mouth and swallows it.

Lutembe seems quite accustomed to a crowd round her. Lazily she lies on the beach, and even raises her head for a photograph. The boys are entranced. This is indeed a new and interesting kind of biology lesson for them. I am sure that it is the kind they should have oftener. One of them impudently flicks a mud pellet at her head to make her demonstrate the movement of her eyelids. After a performance lasting about ten minutes Lutembe heaves her great white belly up on to her short legs, makes a half-turn and crawls back into the lake to await the next visitor and the next piece of fish. She is very fat and hideous. At the Murchison Falls we saw bigger crocodiles, but Lutembe is a good size and must be very ancient. It is likely that she is at least a centenarian.

For many years she has been surrounded by tradition and legend, but it is difficult to find out exactly the part she played in the old tribal life. As far as I could learn she had a great reputation for wisdom and acted as judge in trials by ordeal. The suspected person would be pushed close to Lutembe. If the crocodile bit him, it was assumed that he was guilty and Lutembe's wisdom was applauded. 'Lutembe always knows, she knows the wrong doer', I can imagine them saying. It is probable that Lutembe

153

generally did bite the man; probably the judges would choose a time when she was hungry. It is probable also that she was one of the crocodiles to whom the King's prisoners and criminals were thrown. Old tradition and customs die hard. There is reputed to have been a case, or an attempted case, of trial by ordeal with Lutembe at the lakeside only about ten years ago.

After the diversion of Lutembe, a diversion which no visitor to Uganda should miss, we go on to Entebbe. This is a truly beautiful place with large bungalows set in spacious gardens and with broad lawns sloping in a parklike way to the lake shore. There is no sense of overcrowding as at Kampala. Entebbe is laid out with a spaciousness which seems right for Africa. There is plenty of room in Africa.

On one side of the town are the Botanic Gardens, again open and parklike, with some magnificent trees and clumps of bamboo. They slope down to the lake, and this has been kept well in view when they were planned. Fine specimens of native trees and plants predominate, but there are also many imported plants. In a small dip steps lead down into as cool and charming a little piece of forest as anyone could desire. Over the path hang fine tree ferns; everything is green and luxuriant. In this case it is a controlled luxuriance, but the saying that 'Ars est celare artem' has been applied here with great success.

The lake itself is very blue and soft in colour. Away on the horizon are the even bluer Sesse Islands. It is so large that the term lake seems an understatement. Sea would be more appropriate. Entebbe is cooler than Kampala, since it gets breezes from the lake and must be much the pleasanter place in which to live. However, having two capitals and a division of twenty miles between different branches of Government departments must cause considerable inconvenience, although there is quite a good telephone service between them.

From the town life of Uganda it is well to turn to the country life. Just round the towns, country and town life are becoming amalgamated as in England. There are, as yet, no rows of little villas as there are round Nairobi, and no early morning suburban trains; but there are now many African boys who bicycle several miles daily from their huts to their work in offices, shops and laboratories in Kampala. This seems to be the first stage in the development of the combined town and ever-spreading suburb which has proved so disastrous in England. House boys mostly live on the premises, but retain huts in the country which they visit occasionally. Some lose connection with their country and tribal life entirely, and this presents, perhaps, one of the most difficult problems that confronts East Africa to-day, since their former life was a communal life, and the change to a European individualism is not yet complete; nor is it certain that it would be wholly desirable. So there are now two forces acting upon them in opposite directions, one tending towards the European individualism, the other trying to preserve something of the old communal tribal life.

CHAPTER XII

RED EARTH

BUT the Uganda people are not really a town people. They are essentially a country people. The main unit of social life throughout is still that of the family, and the majority of the people are peasant proprietors, tilling the land with the aid of their families. The individualism, bred by town life, has not yet taken a strong hold in the country. It is still essentially the same rather sleepy, rather peaceful, rather easy-going country dwellers that form the bulk of the people and dominate the land. Kampala seems still an alien growth, not a real part of Uganda. There is still plenty of room in the countryside. I gathered that each family could have a reasonable sized plot of land. By cultivating this land they are easily able to grow enough food to live on. Their essentials of life are luckily still independent of slumps and financial crises. Money is only an extra, something with which to pay taxes and buy luxuries, not an absolute essential of life. Although more and more as the years pass and European civilization takes a stronger hold on the country, money will play a greater and a greater part in their lives. Already it dominates the lives of most of those who live in or near the larger towns. Their old order of life must necessarily pass.

After Elgon our next mountain trip was to the Aberdare range in Kenya. Ford and I drove down from Kampala with Boanerges to meet Edwards and Taylor at Naivasha. They had just come out from England. The journey from Kampala down into Kenya showed us a good piece of the Uganda countryside.

From Kampala the road is hilly, not with big mountains, but with little round green hills. It seemed as if the whole country was made up of them. A very large part of it actually is—only the eastern and northern provinces are flat. A rounded hump seems to be the dominating form in Uganda. From the hills this hump form is carried down to the little round thatched huts, to the women busily tilling the ground, stooping so that their buttocks make a round hump, to the little mounds of red earth on which they plant their sweet potatoes or ground-nuts, and finally to the gigantic round-topped anthills.

Few people and huts are actually visible from the road, and the country seems very underpopulated. It is true that it is sparsely populated, but the majority of the people live back from the roads. In some places, especially near Kampala, the round beehive huts have been replaced with little square mud houses, one-storied, with a tin roof and maybe doors and windows. Although not quite so picturesque, these must be infinitely pleasanter and more hygienic to live in. The beehive huts are naturally very dark inside and generally full of smoke, as there is no form of chimney and the smoke can only get out through the chinks in the roof.

Round the huts are patches of bananas, luscious and green. This perpetual brilliant green is one of the two dominating tones of the country. It is the most abundant. The other is a fiery brick red, which comes from patches of the soil, from the roads and from the anthills. It is an astounding red soil, of so fiery and intense a colour that it might be red hot. Sometimes this wonderful red road runs like a flaming ribbon through banks of luscious green vegetation. I particularly remember one place where it ran down a hillside to the lake. On either side were slopes covered with tall elephant grass; intermingled were a few scarlet kirikiti trees which caught up the intense colour of the road. Down the hill ran this fiery ribbon as the track of some dragon, only to be finally quenched in the deep blue of the lake.

Another picture remains in my mind, and this Somerville has perpetuated for me. It was early morning and the women were still working in the fields. We looked up a little red path to see at the top a pair of huts and a group of bananas. In front of the hut a woman in a vivid blue robe was tilling the red earth, a very perfect symphony of colour. The earth she raised into little mounds on which she planted ground-nuts. The blue woman was bent almost double, in an attitude which no European woman could reach. Her legs were almost straight; the end of her back and her buttocks stuck up as a blue mound rhythmically carrying on the shape of the hills and little huts. She was using the typical 'Jembe' which every African in Uganda uses, a short-handled hoe, with which she pecked at the ground. Beside her a young man was standing, watching her every movement. Such work in the field is traditionally woman's work.

At the edge of the little fields were two anthills, the same vivid scarlet in tone. One had curved over slightly at the top, as if bending in sympathy with the lady of the fields. The earth from these anthills is very hard and also sterile and unfertile, so for the most part they are left undisturbed to grow larger and larger. It was a dominating, an intense, a stimulating landscape. There were no half-tones. It seemed to represent the true, the traditional Uganda, the real Africa as a contrast to the semi-Europeanized life of Kampala.

All the roadside, however, was not red, nor was it all cultivated. There were great dips in which we passed through patches of luxuriant green forest, probably remnants of the primitive forest, which once may have covered the greater part of Uganda and joined with the Ituri forests of the Belgian Congo. The grassland and savannah is largely a secondary growth due to shifting cultivation and grazing. In the forest gigantic lianas fall in rope-like festoons from hundred-foot trees and the floor is covered with a green thicket. Compared with the rain forests of Borneo these patches are like poor relations, stunted and undergrown; but forgetting Borneo they seem full of coolness and dark mystery.

In other dips there are papyrus swamps and small streams. At the edge of the swamp, where the ground becomes a little drier, are clumps of the Phœnix Palm with graceful long plumes.

As we emerge from a dip of forest we are suddenly enveloped in a herd of Uganda cattle which fill the road, padding gently along. They are in charge of a small boy. Some are enormous beasts with blotched brown-and-white flanks, dome-shaped humps and gigantic horns, horns such as are never seen on a beast in England, but which are rather reminiscent of some proud trophy on the walls of a sportsman's shooting lodge. Yet here they are driven placidly along the road by a small boy who whacks at them cheerfully.

Jinja and the source of the Victoria Nile are the next points of interest on our journey. This source is no mere trickle, but a great wide river where we cross it a quarter of a mile below the Ripon Falls. A fine bridge has been built which has two tiers. On one runs the road, on the other the railway line. Incidentally, the bridge is portrayed on the new Uganda stamp with the road ending in mid-river. Below it the river flows, boiling and swirling in a series of rapids. The Ripon Falls themselves, by which the river emerges from Lake Victoria, are not very high or impressive. The whole scene, though, with the swirling water and the blue lake behind, is very pleasing to the eye. Formerly the land all round the base of the Falls was papyrus swamp, but it has been drained and is now used as a golf course and covered with short turf. Every town in Africa where there are a handful of Europeans seems to have a golf course. I never saw an

African playing golf, although they have taken to football with great avidity.

After Jinja the round hills become fewer and lower, until we emerge into the flat country of the Eastern Province, with its thorn acacia scrub and statuesque Borassus palms. These are something like giant carrots, smooth bulging stems surmounted by graceful fronds.

Although cotton is the main export industry of the country, I cannot remember seeing many cotton fields by the side of this road, although in the part of the Eastern Province around Serere, and all round Lake Kioga, much cotton is grown. The finest cotton of all we saw in the country was grown by an Indian farmer. He had planted on a large scale by the edge of the lake in a very fertile spot, employed much labour, and was probably making a good profit.

The cotton in Uganda forms a much branched herb about three or four feet high. If left to itself it would probably become a bigger bush, but after every crop the plants are taken up and burned so as to minimize the insect and fungus pests. In Uganda it is treated as an annual, being sown any time between March and May, or even as late as June, and gathered from October to January. The plants should be covered with large pale pink or creamy mallow-like flowers, and later with silvery-white balls. These are gathered and the cotton thread is torn off the seed by a process known as 'ginning'. Although so much cotton is grown, and so much cotton material is worn by the women, it is noticeable that there is no weaving industry in the country. All the material is imported, the most part from Japan, a little from England. In Nigeria I have heard that there is a big African weaving industry, and it seems a pity that such an industry could not be built up in Uganda, the goods being produced chiefly with a view to home consumption rather than export.

160

Around Jinja the hills take on a lighter, a more uniform shade of green. When we approach closer we see that they are clothed with a dense crop of a tall reed. This is sugar cane. These waving green seas, which cover the hills for several miles, are the main supply of the gigantic Lugezi sugar factory, which is owned and managed by an Indian merchant and has become a vast concern, supplying much of East Africa, and even exporting sugar, until a few years ago when a slump in sugar prices made this no longer profitable. As far as the eye can reach the sugar canes wave, and among them run little miniature railways. On the other side of Jinja there is a second and smaller factory.

The road is so good that we hardly noticed the distance, and it is still well before dark when we arrive at Tororo, where we are to spend the first night. Tororo is renowned for its rock, a great precipitous mass which stands up from the plain and is visible from miles around. At Tororo there is also an aerodrome, and the rock makes an excellent landmark for pilots.

Here there is a good hotel with an English atmosphere and a truly English example of 'Mine Host'. He even has a sign in front of the door. His bar is a fine panelled room and reminds one of some English country town. As a contrast, his dining room is furnished with steel tubing and chromium furniture, which looks very bright and pleasant. The cooking is good, and we feel indeed lucky to find such a comfortable and typically English tavern in a small town in the heart of Africa.

APPENDIX I

ON SOME LEGENDS RELATING TO
THE SOURCES OF THE NILE AND
THE MOUNTAINS OF THE MOON

CLASSICAL legends relating to the sources of the Nile are numerous. Its annual rise made it by far the most interesting river then known. It was also probably the largest, and so its source became a problem which evidently greatly intrigued the ancients. Picturesque though many of these stories and legends are, they are still delightfully vague when related to the actual geography as we know it to-day, and this vagueness, coupled with their romantic name, has caused innumerable speculations as to which of the mountains of Equatorial Africa really constitute the 'Mountains of the Moon'. I fear that I have no new evidence to throw into the controversy and no new startling decision to make, but the legends are so attractive and so picturesque that I feel they have an interest for themselves alone, quite apart from their relation to present-day geography.

Homer conceived of the world as bounded by the encircling ocean. The Nile he traces to the south of Libya, beyond which by the borders of ocean he places the land of the pigmies. Whether he had any actual knowledge of the pigmies of Central Africa or whether he imagined them with the same facility as we believe him to have imagined the Cyclops, it is impossible to say. That is probably the earliest reference to the problem that is still extant. No exact date can be given to Homer, but a very approximate date of 1000 B.C. is often ascribed to him. We hear nothing more of the sources of the Nile for five centuries, and even then Hipparchus had advanced little on Homer in knowledge.

Herodotus, the ancient traveller and historian, is our next informant. In 457 B.C. he visited Egypt and ascended the Nile as far as Elephantinê. In the description of that journey he ascribes no source to the Nile, but only on his return from Elephantinê did he meet the priest of the temple at Sais, who told him the following story, as Herodotus alleges. In Book 2 he writes:

'In all my intercourse with Egyptians, Libyans and Greeks, I have only met one person who pretended to have any knowledge of the sources of the Nile, the priest of the temple at Sais (Sais was a city important in ancient Egypt, situated in the Nile Delta region). He assured me that on this subject he possessed the most unquestionable intelligence, although his assertions never obtained my serious confidence. He informed me, that betwixt Syenê, a city of the Thebais and Elephantinê, there were two mountains, relatively terminating in an acute summit; the name of the one was Crophi, of the other Mophi. He affirmed that the sources of the Nile, which were fountains of unfathomable depth, flowed from the centres of these mountains; that one of these streams divided Egypt, and directed its course to the north; the other in like manner flowed towards the south, through Ethiopia. To confirm his assertion, that the springs were unfathomable, he told me, that Psammetichus, sovereign of the country, had ascertained it by an experiment; he let down a rope of the length of several thousand ogyiæ, but could find no bottom. This was the priest's information, on the truth of which I presume not to determine.'

It appears, therefore, that even Herodotus, who seemed to have acquired something of a reputation for credulity, was doubtful of this story, as well he might be, since he had himself ascended the Nile as far as Elephantinê and knew that the source could have been nowhere near there. Syenê has been identified with Assuan and was situated on the Nile where it crossed from Egypt into Ethiopia. We may note that the name Ethiopia was always used then. Abyssinia is only a comparatively modern name for the country.

There is no satisfactory reason to account for the names 'Crophi' and 'Mophi', which are found nowhere else. It seems more than likely that Herodotus, talking to the priest through an interpreter, misunderstood what was said. It is possible that the two names, which form a pleasant sounding jingle, were invented by the priest or the interpreter, anxious to please an inquisitive stranger.

Strabo, the Greek historian and geographer, who was born about 63 B.C., also visited Egypt and ascended the Nile to Syenê. He comments on Herodotus' story in the following unambiguous and doubtless appropriate words:

'Both Herodotus and others talk much nonsense, adding to their account marvellous tales, to give it, as it were, a kind of tune or rhythm or relish; as, for example, the assertion that the sources of the Nile are in the neighbourhood of the islands near Syenê and Elephantinê (of which there are several) and that at this place its channel has a bottomless depth. The Nile has very many islands scattered along its course, of which some are wholly covered at its risings and others only partly; but the exceedingly high parts of the latter are irrigated by means of screws.' [Probably paddle wheel boats.]

There is, however, some slight information that leads us to suppose that close to Syenê and Elephantinê there was a deep pool or basin in the Nile. Tacitus in his Annals tells of the visit of Germanicus to the spot. 'Germanicus took notice of other wonders, besides, the . . . , the basin excavated to receive the overflowing waters of the Nile and elsewhere again channels so narrow and so profound that no sounding line can reach the bottom.' It may have been to this pool that the priest at Sais was alluding, and that Herodotus falsely thought that he was ascribing to it the source of the Nile. In a footnote to their account of Herodotus' story, Messrs. Cary and Warmington, in their book on ancient explorers, make reference to an inscription of Ptolemais VIII to the effect that 'there was much later a spot called "The Fountain of the Nile" near Elephantinê'. As for the story of Psammetichus, it is related that King Psammetichus II, who reigned from 594 to 589 B.C., sent a mercenary force into Ethiopia as far as Abu Simbel, and Greeks were included, their names having been found scratched on temple statues there. As for the two sharp-pointed peaks, they may possibly refer to the sides of one of the cataracts, but no satisfactory explanation of them can be given.

But that Strabo had some knowledge that the Nile rose in mountains we can be certain from the following statement, although it is probable that it refers chiefly to the Ethiopian source of the Blue Nile.

'Now the ancients depended mostly on conjecture, but the men of later times, having become eye witnesses, perceived that the Nile was filled by summer rains when upper Ethiopia was flooded, and particularly in the region of its furthermost mountains, and that when the rains ceased, the inundation gradually ceased.'

Strabo also records a theory which seems to have been common at the time that the Nile rose in Maurusia, the country which is now called Morocco, and where are the Atlas Mountains.

'Some think that even the sources of the Nile are near the extremities of Maurusia. And they say that in a certain river are found leeches seven cubits long, with gills pierced through with holes, through which they breathe. They also say of this country that it produces a vine so thick that it can hardly be encircled by the arms of two men, and that it yields clusters of about one cubit; and that every herb grows high, and every vegetable, as, for example, arum and dracontium; and the stalks of the staphylini and the hippomarathi and the scolyni grow twelve cubits high and four palms thick. And for serpents also, and elephants and gazelle and similar animals, as also for lions and leopards, the country is a nurse in every way. It also produces ferrets equal in size to cats, and like them, except that their noses project further; and also a great number of apes.'

The Barbary apes are well known, even to-day, from the coast of Morocco. There is, however, in my mind a very faint possibility that the rest of the passage previous to the description of the animals might refer to the Nile sources in Equatorial Africa, and is due rather to faulty orientation in the shape of Africa. The leeches seven cubits long might refer to lampreys, but also might be construed as the first reference to the extraordinary lungfish which are common in the waters of Equatorial Africa. The words 'Staphylini' and 'Hippomarathi' are stated to belong to plants of the umbellifer family, the former being approximately a carrot and the latter a horse-fennel. Now both in Uganda and on the equatorial mountains there are most gigantic and treelike Umbellifers, which would approach the description. Large arums only occur on the mountains, and Dracaenas are abundant both on the mountain and in the moister parts of Uganda.

Pliny the elder also subscribes to the legend of the source in the Atlas Mountains, quoting King Juba of Mauretania as his authority. 'Originem in monte Inferioris Mauretaniæ non procul Oceano habet.'

Aristotle, in the *Meteorologica*, ascribes the source of the Nile to a so-called 'silver mountain'. Æschylus, in the *Prometheus Vinctus*, alludes to the subject. Prometheus directs the unfortunate wanderer Io to go to the 'river Æthiops, along whose verges journey till thou come to the cataract where from the Bybline hills are spilt the holy waters of the Nile'.

H. M. Stanley, the explorer, was much interested in the historical aspect of the sources of the Nile, and in his book, *In Darkest Africa*, he quotes an old paper to show that many of the great figures of history were anxious to discover the source of the Nile, thinking it to be the only great discovery which they could still add to their fame. 'When Alexander the Great consulted the oracle of Jupiter Ammon the first thing he desired to know was whence the Nile sprang, and having camped on the Indus he believed that he had at last succeeded.' 'Lucan makes Cæsar say in his *Pharsalia* that he would readily abandon the design of warring against his country could he be happy enough to see the primal fountain of the Nile.'

Pliny also relates for us the story of the progress up the Nile of two centurions sent by the Emperor Nero, whom he describes most sarcastically:

'I have heard two centurions, whom Emperor Nero (strong lover of truth above all, as he is of other virtues) had sent to investigate the source of the Nile, tell how they travelled a long journey by the time, when furnished with military help by the Ethiopian King and recommended by him to neighbouring kings, they had penetrated to regions beyond his realm. "And indeed," they said, "we came to immense marshes, the outcome of which neither the inhabitants knew nor can anyone hope to know, in such a way are the plants entangled with the waters, not to be struggled through on foot or in a boat, because the marsh, muddy and blocked up, does not admit any unless it is small and holding one person." "There," said one of them, "we saw two rocks, from which a great force of river water came falling," but whether that was the source of or merely an addition of water from below to the Nile . . . do you not believe, dear reader, that whatever it is it rises up from a great lake of the earth.'

There can be little doubt that the centurions encountered the Nile Sudd, the vast papyrus swamps, which to this day form a very considerable barrier to travel in the higher reaches of the Nile.

Ptolemy, A.D. 90 to 168, is our next important authority, and he brings in two new ideas, the lakes and the Mountains of the Moon. In Book 4 he writes: 'Around this bay the Anthropophagi Ethiopians dwell, and from there towards the west are the Mountains of the Moon from which the lakes of the Nile receive snow water; they are located at the extreme limits of the Mountains of the Moon. Moreover, above these are the Rhapsi Ethiopians; the Ichthyophagi Ethiopians dwell in the great bay towards the western Ocean, and towards the south of this to the unknown land are those who are commonly called the Hesperi Ethiopians; towards the east are the Athaca Ethiopians; and more toward the east, adjoining the entire Libyan country, is much Ethiopian land in which elephants are born entirely white, and rhinoceroses and tigers; next to the unknown land of Ethiopia is a region of wide expanse called the Agisymba. This region has many and high mountains near the unknown land, the majority of which are without name.'

All this information was based, as far as we know, on the previous geographical writings of Marinus of Tyre, which are most unfortunately lost, and Marinus apparently based his information largely on the journey of one Diogenes who was blown out of his course down the coast of Africa. Ptolemy quotes the story in Book 1: 'Concerning the voyage from Aromata to Rhapta (Zanzibar or Daar es Salaam) Marinus tells us that a certain Diogenes, one of those who were accustomed to sail to India, having been driven out of his course, and being off the coast of Aramata, was caught by the north wind, and having sailed with Trogloditica on his right, came in twenty-five days to the lake from which the Nile flows, to the south of which lies the promontory of Rhaptum.' This account, though, leaves me at any rate rather uncertain whether Diogenes actually went as far inland as Lake Victoria. It would be a very quick march to do it in twenty-five days, although it would be just possible, and we must not look too closely at that figure. In that case he would probably have seen in the distance Mts. Kenya and Kilimanjaro, and may have thought that their snows fed the Nile. On the other hand, it seems not unlikely that most of the information is based on tales told to Diogenes at the coast. In Ptolemy's map the Moon Mountains are shown as a great range about five hundred miles long, running east and west, south of the equator, and, of course, no such range exists. Various authorities at different times have called into question the authenticity of the maps, suggesting that they are later interpolations to the Ptolemaic text. One author, Mr. Cooley, has even suggested that the whole passage relating to the Mountains of the Moon is a later interpolation to the text, but there does not seem to me any good reason to suppose this.

Throughout the Middle Ages, and, indeed, down to the last century, our information received little alteration, although various maps recorded various positions for the lakes, and, indeed, varied their numbers. But the fundamental idea remained the same. Mr. Cooley, in his little book on Ptolemy and the Nile, published in 1854, also quotes a new and original suggestion, attributing it to one Philostorgius III near the close of the fourth century: 'The Nile rises in the North of Asia, then flowing South, it dives under the Indian Ocean, and running beneath the Erythræan sea, comes forth again at its other side, which is named from the Moon.'

That the Arabs penetrated into East Africa far from the coast during the Dark Ages cannot be denied, and their knowledge of the mountains was probably as great as Ptolemy's, if not greater. They repeatedly refer to the Mountains of Gumr, which has generally been associated with the word 'Kamar', meaning the Moon. It is, however, also possible that it is associated rather with the word 'Komr', which means an object of a pale green colour.

Stanley was particularly interested in the Arab sources of information, and on his return from the African expeditions he found an ancient manuscript in Egypt, much of which appeared to be based on an even older book called *The Explorer's Desire*. He quotes at length from this in his book, *In Darkest Africa;* so I will only mention a very few pieces here.

Abu el Fadel, son of Kadama, wrote:

'As for the Nile, it starts from the mountains of Gumr beyond the Equator, from a source from which flow ten rivers, every five of these flowing into a separate lake, then from each one of these two lakes, two rivers flow out; then all four of these rivers flow into one great lake in the first zone and from this great lake flows out the Nile.'

Later on in the same document we find speculation as to its annual rise.

'Some say that its rise is caused by snows melted in summer, and according to the quantity of snowfall will be the greater or lesser rise. Others say that the rise is caused by the different directions of the winds; that is to say, that when the north wind blows strongly, it stirs up the Mediterranean and pushes the waters thereof backwards so that it overflows the land; and when the south wind blows the Mediterranean ceases to storm, and the waters that were dammed up flow away again.' 'Others say that the rise is caused by fountains upon its banks that have been seen by travellers who have reached to the highest point.'

'Others say that the Nile flows from snowy mountains, and they are the mountains called Kaf. That it passes through the Green Sea, and over gold and silver and emerald and ruby mines, flowing on *ad infinitum* until it reaches the lake of the Zingh and they say were it not to enter into the salt sea and be mixed up with the waters thereof it could not be drunk for great sweetness.'

Again we find 'Some say that people have ascended the mountain, and one of them began to laugh and clap his hands, and threw himself down on the further side of the mountain. The others were afraid of being seized with the same fit and so came back. It is said that those who saw it, saw bright snows like white silver glistening with light. Whoever looked at them became attracted and stuck to them until they died, and this science is called "Human Magnetism".

'It is said that a certain king sent an expedition to discover the Nile sources, and they reached copper mountains, and when the sun rose, the rays reflected were so strong that they were burnt.

Others say that these people arrived at bright mountains like crystal, and when the rays of the sun were reflected they burnt them.' In this connection it is interesting to note the recent development of a copper mine at Kilembe at the foot of Ruwenzori, but there is, as far as I know, no ground for supposing that the copper had been worked earlier.

From the same document I quote the following: 'Mohammed, the prophet of God, says: "The Nile comes out of the Garden of Paradise, and if you were to examine it when it comes out, you would find in it leaves of Paradise".'

The great discoveries of mountains in Equatorial Africa by European explorers in the last century brought forward a flood of identifications of the legendary Mountains of the Moon with various actual mountains, especially with Ruwenzori. H. M. Stanley, the Duke of the Abruzzi, and Sir Harry Johnston supported this strongly, basing their claim on the assumption that Ruwenzori is the only one of the Equatorial Mountains which can in any way be considered a range, that its long stretch of glaciers would be far more conspicuous than the snow dome of Kilimanjaro or the peaks of Kenya, and that the waters from its snows do really feed the Nile and are among its furthermost sources. There is no doubt that the glaciers on all these mountains have been considerably larger in recent geological ages than they are at present. Our own experiences on Ruwenzori showed us that the Nyamgasani glacier had retreated very recently leaving a bare expanse of rock. So it seems to me probable that even at so very recent a time geologically as two thousand years ago the glaciers and snowfields were larger and the whiteness of the mountains more conspicuous than at present.

Actually the uttermost source of the Nile is generally acknowledged to be the Kagera river, which rises in the Mufumbiro volcano country to the north-east of Lake Kivu, and some have suggested that these mountains have the strongest claim to be 'The Mountains of the Moon', but they can hardly be considered as a range as can Ruwenzori, and only a few of them have any permanent snow.

To the south of Lake Victoria, away from the mountain country, is the country of the Unyamwazi, the people of the Moon. It has been suggested that this name may have had something to do with the origin of the name 'Mountains of the Moon', although the country they now live in could in no wise represent it. That country, though, might have been on the trade route from the coast into the centre of Africa, and the coastal Arabs might have heard of the Mountains through them.

In spite of all these facts and suppositions, it seems to me very doubtful whether Ptolemy had knowledge more definite than that there were snow mountains in the centre of Africa, and that their snows fed the Nile. If so, it would be natural for him to mark the mountain range as running east and west, that is at right angles to the main course of the Nile, which he conceived as rising in it. If, however, we really want to allot to any one range the proud title, it seems that Ruwenzori is the most suitable.

Recently, Dr. Noel Humphreys, who has travelled much on Ruwenzori, has tentatively put forward an interesting theory to connect the Crophi and Mophi of Herodotus with Emin and Gessi, the two most northern of the snow peaks of Ruwenzori and the lake between them, the source of the Ruamuli river, with the Fountain of the Nile. If we feel able to pass over the fact of the erroneous position of the peaks as described between Elephantinê and Syenê, and disconnect Crophi and Mophi from the rest of the story, this theory would be very pleasing. If, on the other hand, we rather agree with Strabo's opinion of Herodotus' story, this latest and attractive theory must needs fall with Herodotus.

BIBLIOGRAPHY

Æschylus. *Prometheus Vinctus*, l. 838.

Aristotle. *Meteor*, Book I, Chap. 13, l. 21.

Bunbury. *History of Ancient Geography*, p. 612.

Cary and Warmington. *Ancient Explorers*.

Cooley, W. D. *Claudius Ptolemy and the Nile*, 1854.

Filippi. *Ruwenzori*.

Herodotus, Book II.

Humphreys, Dr. Noel. *Geographical Journal*, December 1933.

Johnston, Sir H. H. *The Nile Quest*.

Ptolemy, translated Stevenson, published 1932. Book IV, Chap. 8; Book I, Chap. 9.

Stanley, H. M. *In Darkest Africa*, Vol. II.

Strabo. *Geography*, trans. by H. L. Jones, 17. 1. 5. and 17. 1. 52.

Tacitus Annals, II, 61.

APPENDIX II

SOME NOTES ON POSSIBLE GARDEN PLANTS FROM THE MOUNTAINS OF EQUATORIAL AFRICA

WHEN we consider the very striking and decorative characteristics of many of the plants from the Equatorial mountains of East Africa, it seems surprising that not a single one of them is in general cultivation in England to-day, either as a hardy plant or as a greenhouse plant. Coming from altitudes very similar to those at which some of our most successful garden plants have been collected in the Himalayas we might have expected a different story. It is true that seed collected from these mountains has been rare in England, but even so, a tradition has grown up that these plants are almost impossible of cultivation in normal English gardens. There is no doubt that many of them are difficult, but I do not think that by any means all of them are impossible or even specially difficult. I hope that the results which we have had in Surrey from my own seeds, and which have resulted elsewhere, will show this sufficiently.

Before we consider the plants in detail I would like to describe very briefly the vegetational zones of each mountain and some of the environmental factors under which the plants grow. On each of these mountains the vegetational zones are very well marked. In every case the change from one zone to another is abrupt, and in most cases each species is only found in one zone, or even within a narrower altitudinal range than is represented by the whole zone. In the Nyamgasani valley of Ruwenzori the zones were roughly as follows.

6,000 ft. to 7,500 ft. *Mixed Evergreen rain forest.*

This forest is particularly thick and luxuriant beside the streams. It cannot, however, compare in grandeur with the rain forest we had seen in Borneo. There are comparatively few large trees. I believe that there are more in the Bujuku and other eastern valleys, where the forest probably obtains a greater luxuriance. In this zone, as far as we could discover, the temperature never descended to freezing-point, and so there is little hope that the plants would be generally hardy except in the very sheltered and mild parts of England. The majority are more tropical than temperate in appearance. Conspicuous in the undergrowth are the tree ferns, *Cyathca* sp., and the wild bananas, *Musa ensete*. Beside the streams and in other damp places grows a very fine pink balsam, *Impatiens* sp.

From 7,500 ft. to 10,000 ft. extends the bamboo forest. In the lower zones the bamboos are very large, reaching a height of more than 50 ft., but between 9,000 ft. and 10,000 ft. they decrease gradually in size until they are no more than 15 ft. to 20 ft. in height. Around the streams the bamboo forest is partly replaced by a very luxuriant evergreen forest with *Podocarpus* and other large trees. In such places we found the magnificent scarlet Amaryllid, *Choananthus cyrtanthiflorus*, and a fine green and white *Arisæma*. The upper layers of the soil in this zone had a medium covering of humus and the soil was mostly acid to some depth, although it did not have the inky-black appearance of the soil in the Ericetum (heather forest) above.

Almost exactly at 10,000 ft. there is an abrupt change into the heather forest zone, the Ericetum, that zone which makes Ruwenzori such a peculiar mountain. In Borneo we had found a similar abrupt transition between the evergreen rain forest and the moss forest, and I believe that such a character is common in tropical mountain floras.

Some have called all the Ericetum a subalpine zone and the bare rocks higher up alpine. Others have called all this zone alpine, but the term does not seem to me wholly appropriate. Between 10,000 ft. and 13,000 ft. the heathers, *Erica arborea* and *Philippia Johnstonii*, are very large, being often 40 ft. or 50 ft. in height and having trunks several feet in circumference. In this zone is the chief growth of the arborescent senecios and the giant lobelias. On all the trees, and covering the ground thickly, is a very dense growth of mosses, liverworts and lichens. In the Nyamgasani valley we found the Ericetum divided into an upper and a lower zone. Between 10,000 ft. and 11,000 ft. the undergrowth is chiefly composed of a very dense growth of *Mimulopsis Elliotii*, an Acanthaceous plant with white flowers and a rather unpleasant smell. Often this thicket reached five or six feet in height. Intermingled with the *Mimulopsis* was an attractive small flowered deep red balsam, a fine *Rubus* with pale pink flowers and silvery white stems, *Peucedanum Kerstenii*, an almost arborescent Umbellifer with very finely divided fernlike foliage, and several species of *Helichrysum* (Everlastings).

Above the *Mimulopsis* comes a zone where the undergrowth below the tree heathers is more varied, but where a silvery leaved Alchemilla of one to two feet in height is dominant. Above

13,000 ft. the tree heathers diminish very much in size until at about 13,600 ft. they are replaced by a scrub of the straw-coloured everlasting, *Helichrysum Stuhlmannii*, which has already occurred with more moderation in the flora since 11,000 ft. and whose leaves display an increasing woolliness as the altitude increases. In places this scrub is four or five feet deep, and so thick that it is extremely tiring to battle one's way through for more than a few yards, and it is really necessary to cut a path.

In the Ericetum the soil is an inky-black, waxy, somewhat gravelly peat, which is very acid. There is, as far as we found, no fully-developed podsol, as is often developed in heathlands in Europe. While practically all this zone is very damp, in many places there are large open patches of regular swamp in which raised tussocks of *Carex runsorrensis* are dominant. In these open patches of swamp the green spiky *Lobelia Bequaertii* with the large purple rosettes is found, while in the forest, and in drier open patches, the silvery-blue *Lobelia Wollastonii* is common. The latter species ascends higher than the tree heathers and is found up to 14,700 ft., where there is little other vegetation than black lichen covering the rocks and an occasional tuft of grass. The arborescent senecios also are found both in the heather forest and in the open places up to 14,500 ft.

The environmental factors under which this extraordinary vegetation has developed are undoubtedly complex. They certainly include a very high humidity, in the case of Ruwenzori an almost perpetual damp season with only very occasional dry spells. This fact may be due partly to the exposed situation and great height of the mountain and partly to the influence of the great Ituri forests on its western side. A high altitude is combined with a high ultra-violet light intensity due both to the factors of the tropical position and the height. This light factor may, however, be somewhat masked by the very frequent mists which cover the mountain.

All these factors, the high humidity, the perpetual dampness, the high altitude and the possible high ultra-violet light intensity, are also combined with a low temperature, varying little throughout the year, and a very acid soil. These two later factors would tend to restrict growth, and their influence can be seen in the very short internodes of the arborescent senecios, the giant lobelias and the almost arborescent Peucedanum. The great luxuriance of foliar growth combined with ultimate size may partly owe its existence to the former factors combined with the lack of definite seasons. On Ruwenzori all the year is a growing season.

On Mount Elgon there seem to be two short but definite dry seasons in the year. Unlike Ruwenzori, which is made up of very ancient rocks, Mt. Elgon is an extinct volcano, and has a large expanse of open grassland above 10,000 ft., very similar to Dartmoor except for the tree heaths and the giant senecios and lobelias. On Elgon, however, the senecios and most of the species of lobelia are found in dampish patches and close to streams. The same is noticeable on Mt. Kenya and the Aberdare Mountains, which have somewhat similar expanses of moorland to Mt. Elgon and are also extinct volcanoes. In this grassland are found numerous little bulbous plants which are quite absent from Ruwenzori, and the flora is considerably richer in numbers of species. Although there are patches of very acid black bogland on Elgon it is probable that the general ground is not nearly so acid as on Ruwenzori. Up to 10,000 ft. there is much the same sequence of mixed evergreen and then bamboo forest, although on Elgon now much of the original forest has been cleared and a scrub of Everlastings has grown up in its place. We have found that plants from Mt. Elgon seem generally more vigorous in growth and more adaptable to the conditions of this country than are plants from Ruwenzori.

Although in their native habitat many of the plants must withstand prolonged periods of frost, it has been found that in this country they are happiest in the south and west, particularly in the west of Scotland, where the weather is mild and, probably even more important, the atmospheric humidity is high. It has been found possible, though, to winter successfully out of doors in Surrey, just with the aid of hand cloches, four different species of giant lobelia, which are still in the rosette stage, but all of which are flourishing. In this country the plants seem to grow much faster in the winter than in the summer. Possibly the heat, combined with the lower atmospheric humidity of the summer months, has a retarding effect on the growth of plants such as these, which are used to a more uniformly cold climate and a high humidity. Another factor in the successful cultivation of these plants seems to be the provision of ample root space and also an absence of root disturbance. For the most part they seem to do better in the open than under glass.

Among the many plants of the mountains the following seemed to be some of those most interesting for horticultural purposes.

Giant Lobelias

These species belong to the *Rhynchopetalum* series of the genus Lobelia, and are found on all the East African mountains, both in the forest and alpine zones. A full account of the group will be found in a paper by Miss E. A. Bruce, in the Kew Bulletin, No. 2, 1934, so I will only give some short notes here from my personal experience of them.

Lobelia gibberoa

This is the largest species of all, and is the only species common to all the mountains, ranging from 6,500 ft. to 10,000 ft., but not emerging into the alpine zone. It is really a plant of the forest glade and of the forest edge. On Mt. Elgon we found it in the bamboo forest at 9,000 ft. Some of the plants were in flower and had reached a height of 29 ft. A more usual height is 15 ft. to 20 ft. The flowers form a dense raceme often ten feet in length. Unfortunately they are greenish-white in colour and partially hidden by linear green pendulent bracts which are larger than the flowers.

This species grows fairly easily from seed and has several times been raised in England. It has recently flowered after six years' growth at Kew in the temperate house. Being a plant of the forest, it will not stand any frost, even though it may be protected with bracken. But in Surrey we have found it easy to grow in a cool greenhouse, moving the plants outside for the summer, and in two years it has attained a height of four and a half feet from seed. The leaves are very large and form a loose rosette on the top of a lanky stem. They have a prominent purple midrib and purple venation which gives them their chief attraction. Its bulk and its coarseness of growth make this probably the least attractive and interesting of the giant lobelias from the horticultural viewpoint. It is, however, probably the easiest to grow, provided that there is sufficient room to winter it in a cool greenhouse and that it can be given ample space.

Lobelia aberdarica

Grows abundantly in open swamp by Bulambuli stream at 9,500 ft. on Mt. Elgon, on the Aberdare Mountains and on Mt. Kenya. Forms a close rosette of slightly fleshy leaves on a short stem never more than two feet from the ground, and a rather slender flower spike up to six feet in height. The flowers are pale blue and are visible between the green bracts.

This is definitely a water-loving plant, and we manage to grow it quite successfully in a small peat bog at the edge of a concrete tank in Surrey. In winter it has the protection of a glass cloche and has so far been unharmed.

Lobelia elgonensis

Mt. Elgon, from 11,000 ft. to 13,500 ft., growing chiefly in swampy places. This species forms a very large and closely packed rosette of green, somewhat fleshy leaves, only very slightly raised above the ground. At the base of each leaf, and generally also in the centre of the rosette, is a slightly gelatinous watery mixture. Often a single rosette may be over two feet in diameter. This plant forms a stout obelisk-like spike up to six feet in height. The flowers are deep blue and can be seen between the stout green bracts which stick horizontally out from the stem. *L. sattimae*, from the Aberdare Mountains, and *L. keniensis*, from Mt. Kenya, are extremely similar in general appearance.

Lobelia Bequaertii

This species is found in the open carex swamps from 11,000 ft. to 14,000 ft. on Ruwenzori, and belongs to the same series as *L. elgonensis*, to which its appearance is rather similar. The rosette, however, is purplish where that of *L. elgonensis* is rich green. The leaves are almost glabrous, and when it is damp the rosettes present a magnificent glistening purple appearance. Both the rosettes and the flower spike are slightly larger than those of *L. elgonensis*, the spike often rising to eight or nine feet. The flowers are deep purplish blue, a very rich colour. This is an exceptionally fine plant, and, I think, one of the most decorative of all the giant lobelias. In Surrey we have both it and *L. elgonensis*, growing in a small peat bog at the edge of a small pond, and they are only protected by a cloche in winter. *L. elgonensis* seems slightly more vigorous and easier of growth than *L. Bequaertii*, and several plants of it have also survived the winter in the ordinary sandy garden soil without any cloche protection. Mr. McDouall reports from Logan (close to Stranraer) that he does not find *L. Bequaertii* completely hardy, but hopes that *L. elgonensis* may yet succeed.

Lobelia Wollastonii

This species is found abundantly on Ruwenzori in the heather forest zone, and in the more open alpine zone above from 11,000 ft. up to 14,700 ft. It also occurs on the Birunga Mountains and is, I think, the finest of all the lobelias when in flower. The flowers are a delicate shade of powder blue in colour and emerge between the long woolly bracts, which are densely covered with a greyish-blue pubescence, so that the whole spike, often 15 ft. in height, is pale silvery blue in appearance.

Unfortunately, this magnificent plant is not at all vigorous in growth in England and does not appear nearly so easy of cultivation as some of the other species mentioned. It is just possible that there may be difficulties connected with mycorrhiza. Mr. McDouall reports that it is not hardy at Logan, nor have we managed yet to maintain it out of doors in Surrey, although on Ruwenzori it has often been photographed half covered with snow and with icicles hanging from the tips of its leaves. Although it often grows in very damp places on Ruwenzori it is definitely not a plant of the peat bogs as is *L. Bequaertii*, and a plant tried in my little peat bog here soon died.

Lobelia Telekii

Mt. Elgon, Aberdare Mountains and Mt. Kenya, 11,000 ft. to 14,000 ft. This plant belongs to the same series as *L. Wollastonii*, but its bracts are green rather than grey-blue, and as they are very long they largely hide the blue flowers and give the whole spike a shaggy appearance. It produces a close rosette and a fairly stout spike often five or six feet in height.

This is the only species of giant lobelia we found which did not seem to grow at all in damp places. It seemed rather to be associated generally with rocky ground, although it also occurred in grassy places. In England it appears to be one of the easiest to grow and to be fairly hardy, having wintered for two years out of doors in Surrey. Mr. McDouall also reports that it is hardy at Logan.

Arborescent Senecios

With the lobelias these form the most striking element in the flora of the higher zones of the Equatorial mountains. They are, however, probably less suitable for cultivation in this country owing to the long gaunt woody stems which most species form. Also their growth in England seems much less hardy and vigorous than the lobelias. Mr. McDouall reports from Logan that they are delicate with him when young, but appear to get hardy when large.

Originally all the arborescent senecios on all the mountains were thought to be only variants of a single species, *S. Johnstonii*, but now, owing to the work of Mr. A. D. Cotton, of Kew, and others, a number of separate species have been identified and a zonal series prepared for each mountain, ranging from the thin-leaved, almost glabrous, species with long ray florets of the forest zone to the more dwarf species with thick leaves covered with silvery pubescence and possessing no ray florets, which is characteristic of the highest zones.

The general appearance of the plants will best be seen from the photographs. On the top of a thick woody trunk is a large rosette of vast, somewhat cabbage-like leaves, often more than two feet in length. For the sake of its rosette alone these senecios would be most decorative plants, especially the higher species, where the leaves are covered with a dense white tomentum, giving them a silvery appearance. The flower spikes are usually very large, often three or more feet in height and bearing hundreds of capitula. In flower, the lower species, which have long ray florets, are the most handsome. It is not known how old the plants must be before they flower, and as far as I know none have yet been flowered in this country. Our measurements on Mt. Elgon showed that most of the species did not flower until they were nearly five feet in height, and I think that it is unlikely that this represents less than five years' growth, and very probably more.

For horticultural purposes I think that the dwarf *Senecio brassica* from Mt. Kenya, or *S. brassicaeformis*, a somewhat similar species from the Aberdare Mountains, would be the most valuable. This plant does not form a long woody trunk, and the rosette is almost sessile on the ground. The leaves are packed closely together and are thickly covered with a close silvery-white indumentum. The flowering spike rises to a height of four or five feet, the ray florets are moderately long, and all the stem of the spike and the peduncles are covered with the thick silvery-white hair. For some time we had several plants of this species growing quite vigorously here in Surrey, but, unfortunately, they have now all died. *S. brassica*, like most of the arborescent senecios, is definitely a water-loving plant, and is found chiefly in boggy places from 11,000 ft. to 14,500 ft. Another rather dwarf and very attractive species is *Senecio alticola*, from the Birunga Mountains, but this does not possess long ray florets like *S. brassica*.

Helichrysums (Everlastings)

There are very many attractive everlastings on these mountains, several attaining the size of large shrubs up to five or six feet in height (*H. Stuhlmannii*, of Ruwenzori). If they could be established in this country I am sure that many of them would be considered an improvement on those already cultivated, both from size and colour of flower and from their graceful habit of growth, which is not nearly so stiff as that of many of the cultivated species. Unfortunately, they have not so far proved very easy of growth in this country and they are very susceptible to insect attacks and damage. The majority of the species have sticky leaves or else have long white indumentum covering the stems and leaves, and this is inclined to become a nest of aphids, etc.

One species, *H. Guilelmii*, from the heather forests of Ruwenzori, is most attractive, having shaggy silvery hairs often several inches in length surrounding as a web the stem and leaves. The capitula are borne in a large corymb and are a delicate pink in colour. We had this plant in cultivation here, but unfortunately have now lost it. The only species we now have is *H. argyrocotyle*, also from the heather forests of Ruwenzori, a lanky branched plant up to three or four feet in height, with sticky leaves and large corymbs of creamy capitula. On the mountains we did not notice anything peculiar about this plant, but in this country it has developed a strong volatile oil, giving a distinct smell as of ether when anyone brushes against the plant. Although this species must withstand some frost on Ruwenzori, we found that here plants in the open were killed off absolutely at the first frost. The most successful plants of this species that I have seen raised from our seed are in the Botanic Gardens at Glasnevin, Dublin, where I understand that they are constantly sprayed with a mild insecticide.

Another attractive species is the little *H. Meyeri-Johannis* from the alpine moorlands of Elgon. It has a creeping stem which often runs underground and puts up large pink flowers cupped in silvery-grey leaves, and only rising a few inches from the ground. It seems to be a very variable plant, but its dwarf forms would be delightful plants for the rock garden or alpine house. I do not know at present of their cultivation in England. Mr. McDouall has raised a certain number of Helichrysums at Logan, but he writes that they are not a real success.

Impatiens (Balsams)

This genus is well represented on these mountains, and several of the species are very fine plants indeed. Perhaps the finest of all is the big white *Impatiens elegantissima* from the lower zones of Mt. Elgon. This plant grows often to a height of six or seven feet, and produces large white flowers, streaked with deep crimson in the centre and floating on the ends of long petioles like great white butterflies, or like the great *Phalaenopsis grandiflora*, one of the finest orchid species of the Philippines and East Indies. Often the flowers are over two inches wide, while the spur may be three or four inches in length. This species forms underground tubers like the dahlia, and it is possible that in England it might be treated satisfactorily in the same way. In our cool greenhouse in Surrey it has made considerable growth, although it has not flowered. Mr. McDouall reports that it is hardy at Logan.

In the evergreen forest, and in the bamboo zone of Ruwenzori, grows a very fine shell-pink Impatiens with flowers often an inch and a half to two inches across, although not so large as the white *I. elegantissima*. It has the same 'butterfly' form of flower with wide winglike lateral petals. This plant has grown satisfactorily in a cool greenhouse in Surrey and has flowered almost continuously for the past year, including throughout the winter. The flowers are rather variable in size and colour, but the best of them make it, in my opinion, a very fine plant. The stems, which reach a height of three and a half to four feet, are deep crimson in colour. Unfortunately it is not hardy, although it seems happy out of doors during the summer in a slightly shady position.

Hypericums (St. John's Wort)

Both dwarf creeping Hypericums with little flowers and shrubby, almost treelike, Hypericums with large flowers are found on these mountains. It is the latter which I would like to see introduced into English gardens. In the commonest species, *H. lanceolatum* from Mt. Elgon, the flowers are about the same size as those of the commonly grown *H. calycinum*, the stigma and ovary is a handsome crimson, while the flowers are borne abundantly and the plant grows to the size of a small tree, often twenty or more feet in height. The foliage is evergreen and very similar to that of the commonly cultivated white Veronica. We have a plant of the highest form of this species growing here in Surrey, and it has now survived two winters out of doors, although it has not yet flowered. But in my opinion the finest Hypericum of all, the finest Hypericum I have seen anywhere, is *H. Bequaertii*, from the heather forests of Ruwenzori. This plant also attains the size of a small tree and bears its flowers pendent at the ends of short branches. Unlike the other members of the genus, these do not open flat, but are cup shaped like small tulips hanging from the branches. The outer petals are deep orange. Unfortunately, this species has not so far proved as vigorous in growth as *H. lanceolatum*, but it is in cultivation.

Kniphofias (Red-hot Pokers)

There are several species of Kniphofia on these mountains, and although none of them are as showy as the commonly cultivated hybrids, many of them are attractive plants and well worth cultivation. One of them, *K. Snowdenii*, from Mt. Elgon, is in cultivation in England and is even now to be found in a few nurserymen's catalogues. It seems to be generally hardy. The flowers are yellow and are borne in a loose raceme two or three feet in height. The plant somewhat resembles a giant Lachenalia.

Canarina Eminii

The genus *Canarina* belongs to the order Campanulaceæ, and only one species, *C. campanulata* from the Canary Islands, is at present generally cultivated in this country. *C. Eminii* grows as an epiphyte on Mt. Elgon between 6,000 ft. and 9,000 ft. The branches and leaves are glaucous and pendulent. At the end are large pale orange bell-shaped flowers lined with deep crimson. Inside the bells is a large club-shaped stigma like a clapper. This plant is easily cultivated in a cool greenhouse in this country, and forms a permanent fleshy tuberous root. After flowering it quickly dies down, and we dry it off like a dahlia tuber and start it into growth early the next spring. *C. Eminii* has a naturally graceful habit of growth which combines with the beautiful flowers and the ease of cultivation to make it a valuable plant. During the summer it can be planted outside. It grows easily from seed.

Choananthus cyrtanthiflorus (sometimes described as C. Wollastonii).

A monotypic Amaryllid genus from the bamboo forest zone of Ruwenzori. This fine plant bears scarlet drooping bell-shaped flowers in large clusters around a stem about eighteen inches in height. Although still little known here it is in cultivation, and a plant received an award of merit in 1928 from the Royal Horticultural Society. It is figured in a fine coloured plate in the *Botanical Magazine*, CLVIII, Pt. 1, and is reported easy of cultivation under cool greenhouse conditions.

Bulbous Plants

On Mt. Elgon particularly there are numerous small bulbous species belonging to the genera *Crinum, Romulea, Hesperantha Gladiolus, Oenostachys*, some of which I now have in cultivation in a cool greenhouse in Surrey and which seem desirable. *Crinum Johnstonii* has bulbs the size of a football, long strap-shaped leaves, and a fine large flower spike about three feet in height and bears several large white flowers prominently streaked with mauve down the centre of each petal. The brilliant scarlet-flowered form of *Gladiolus quartinianus*, from the alpine zone of the Aberdares and Mt. Kenya, is also a most attractive plant and very rich in colour. *Oenostachys dicroa* is a curious plant from Elgon. Its corms and habit of growth are similar to those of a Gladiolus. The flowers are small and are shielded by large bracts which are generally a deep mauve in colour. Major F. C. Stern has flowered this plant at Highdown in Sussex, but has reported that the bracts were green and showed no trace of mauve coloration. It seems as if this might be a physiological character rather than a purely systematic one.

Epiphytic orchids are not very plentiful on these mountains, and we found none of possible horticultural value. Terrestrial orchids are common and several are attractive. The finest is, perhaps, *Disa Stairsii*, which has a fine deep pink spike and is common on all the mountains in boggy places. Unfortunately, it is not easy of cultivation in this country.

There are several umbellifers which we thought attractive, in particular *Peucedanum Kerstenii*, an almost arborescent species from the heather forests of Ruwenzori, with very fine fern-like foliage, and *Heracleum elgonense*, with creamy flowers, from the higher zone of Mt. Elgon. Mr. McDouall had *Peucedanum Kerstenii* growing at Logan, but reports that it was not a success. There are no gentians on these mountains, but the large-flowered, dwarf, white *Swertia* which we found on the Aberdares seemed to me a most attractive plant, and I regret that I have not got it growing here. *Delphinium macrocentrum*, with its gorgeous electric-blue flowers, is another plant which I would like to be able to grow but have not so far been successful. From Ruwenzori the rampant creeper, *Thunbergianthus*, would be desirable for the large, cool greenhouse or the orangery, but none of the seeds we collected have germinated, and other attempts to introduce it have failed. There is also a large golden-flowered *Sedum* about 11,000 ft. on Ruwenzori, which I would like to have been able to introduce. Near the foot of several of the mountains we also found plants such as *Gloriosa superba* and *G. virescens* and *Haemanthus multiflorus*, but these are not elements in the mountain flora and are known in this country.

Although the chief plants of these mountains are by now known, I am sure that there are many which could be profitably introduced into English gardens. There is a possibility also that the second and third generations raised from seed entirely grown in England might prove more hardy and better adapted to English conditions than the first generation.

ITINERARY

DURING the expedition visits were paid to the following mountains:

Aug. 1934 — Mt. Elgon, Uganda side (Ford, Somerville, Synge, accompanied by G. L. R. Hancock and G. C. Hansford, mycologist to the Uganda Government).

Sept. 1934 — Mt. Elgon, Sipi (Somerville and Synge).

Oct. 1934 — Aberdare Mts., Kinangop end (Edwards, Taylor, Ford, and Synge).

Nov. 1934 — Birunga Volcanoes (Edwards, Taylor, Ford, and Synge, accompanied by E. G. Gibbins, of the Uganda Medical Department).

Dec. 1934–Jan. 1935 — Ruwenzori, Namwamba Valley (Edwards and Taylor, accompanied for short periods by E. G. Gibbins, George Oliver, and Mr. T. H. E. Jackson, of Kitale).

Ruwenzori, Nyamgasani Valley (Somerville and Synge, accompanied by D. R. Buxton, who was acting as a special locust investigator in East Africa).

Feb.–March 1935 — Mt. Elgon, Kenya side (Edwards and Taylor, accompanied by T. H. E. Jackson).

April–May 1935 — Mt. Kenya, N.W. slopes (Hancock and Synge, accompanied by four African students and Mr. Adrian van dér Westhuizen, of Nanyuki, Kenya).

May 1935 — Mt. Elgon, Uganda side (Synge).

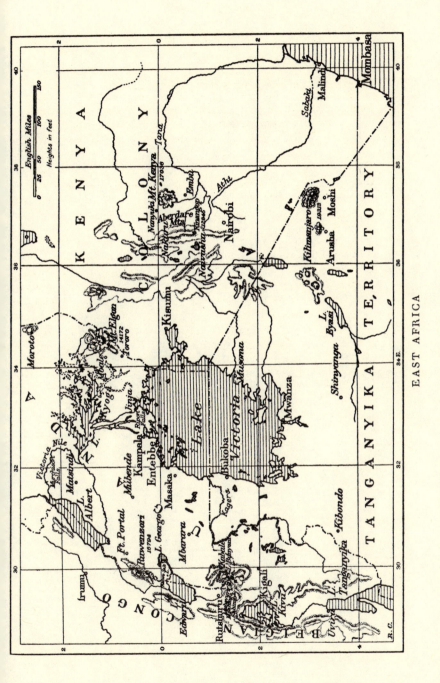

EAST AFRICA

INDEX